GROWING UP INSIDE OUT

Cheryl Thompson Beckett, Ph.D.

in collaboration with
B. J. Barton

Higher States Publishing

Published by
Higher States Publishing
1917 Sheely Drive
Fort Collins, CO 80524

Copyright©1994 by Cheryl Thompson Beckett

Passages and chart from Higher Stages of Human Development,
edited by C. N. Alexander and E. J. Langer, reprinted with
permission from Oxford University Press. Charts in the Appendix
from Scientific Research on Maharishi's Transcendental Meditation
and TM-Sidhi Program, were reproduced with permission from
MIU Press.

Brain Gym®is a registered trademark of the Educational
Kinesiology Foundation.

Trancendental Meditation®and TM® are registered service marks
of the World Plan Executive Council--United States, a nonprofit
educational organization. Maharishi International University®, and
MIU® are service marks of Maharishi International University.

ISBN 0-9642255-0-6

CONTENTS

LIST OF FIGURES

This book is dedicated to the teachers in my life:

My parents
Dr. Gerald Benson
Winifred Reynolds
Reverend Lloyd Peterson
Jesus Christ
Maharishi Mahesh Yogi
Buddha
Mohammed
Robert Fulghum
Dr. Deepak Chopra

Preface

Within the content of this book, it is my sincere desire to give a glimpse of Life's process as I perceive it. Since I was very young, I have had a sense of being a part of a much larger whole. I remember the ecstasy of being in church with my parents at age five and feeling embraced by some awesome wholeness. I remember the minister in my hometown church saying God wasn't definable. The minute you felt you understood Him, you would discover some new aspect.

I have found that true. For me, Life grows in ever-expanding spheres. This book has given me the opportunity to present my perspective on that. It also has brought me to the need to uncover the developmental tasks that will make the mental, emotional, physical, and spiritual growth a deliberate design rather than a default.

I am truly grateful and deeply indebted to my long-time friend and writer/editor, B. J. Barton. Our journey has covered thirty years. Her support, trust, and confidence, began when her daughter was enrolled in my preschool.

I would like to thank the artists who contributed their work to this effort: Polly Capalungo for the cover design and Marc Coen for the additional drawings. I would also like to thank Perrie McMillen for her assistance with material on the back cover.

I trust that many of you, the readers, will be my next teachers as you ask the questions that will continue your developmental process and mine.

Cheryl Thompson Beckett

Chapter 1

It's All About Balance

After I completed my college degree, I felt that I knew about the world. I had goals and ideas about what I was going to do. Then I attended a conference that had monumental impact on my life, and I was transformed by the feelings and concepts that I encountered there. The world I had known before I attended that conference no longer existed. In fact, what I experienced was a change of consciousness that restructured and redefined what I knew. The workshop leader, by the way, was Robert Fulghum, and his book, *All I Ever Needed to Know I Learned in Kindergarten* showed up on my desk some nineteen years later. What a facilitator for change he was in my life!

From that transforming experience I went back to my preschool and made a lot of changes. These changes stayed with me and evolved as I moved through the days, months, and years. I believe that this new consciousness on my part allowed many children to grow with feelings of self worth, self acceptance and self confidence that they may not have known otherwise.

I found it isn't so much what we *do* with children, but how we *be* with children that is important. It's the *being* that structures my attention and affects their doing. The way we conceptualize children, ourselves, and our role in working with children, makes an extraordinary difference in the teaching and learning process.

One day shortly after that conference I sat on the floor with Amanda beside me. She was playing with a piece of building material - a small board with holes that could be used to put nuts and bolts on it. But Amanda wasn't using it that way. She was using it to comb my hair. She would run that piece of wood over my hair. Then she would look at me and say, "Oh, that looks nice," mess my hair up, and start all over again.

1

Amanda obviously enjoyed this game of make believe. While we played like this, a wonderful little girl named Shannon stood off to the side and watched the process we were going through. Thinking that she might want to join us, I said to her, "Shannon, come on over."

"Oh, no," she said, but she still stood and watched. Soon Amanda was on to something else and I asked Shannon again if she wanted to be my hair dresser, but she said no.

The next day Shannon walked up to Amanda and handed her the piece of wood that Amanda had been using to comb my hair and said "Be a hair dresser." Amanda came to me and we went through the whole process again. Shannon continued to watch, I offered to have her join us, and she refused. This happened for two or three days running. Shannon would never join us but she watched almost wistfully as we went through our little ritual. On about the fourth day, Shannon kept one of the pieces of wood in her hand, but still wouldn't join us.

The next day Amanda wasn't there, but Shannon was still processing this whole event. I sat down on the floor, and she had the piece of wood in her hand, and I said, "Are you going to be my hair dresser today, Shannon?"

She picked up her hand as if she were going to touch my head, but she did it ever, ever so cautiously, almost as if I was going to strike her as she was doing that. She moved as if she didn't know where the piece of wood was going to touch my head. She went over my hair cautiously and, when she was done, I said, "O.K. should we mess it up and start over again?" Then she smiled, giggled a little bit, and we messed it up and she "combed" it again.

For the next two weeks, every time Shannon was in preschool we went through this same ritual. She was absolutely delighted to be able to comb my hair.

I didn't understand this interaction until a short time later when my husband and I went over to Shannon's home to talk with her father about some business. We were sitting in the living room when Shannon entered the room. My husband was talking with Shannon's Dad and I invited Shannon to come over and get up on my lap. She did this very reluctantly, but once she

2

was up, she shifted herself and snuggled in as if she was going to stay for a very long time. About this time her Dad noticed Shannon was in my lap, and he said, "Shannon, get down and go to your room. We are having a talk."

The hurt look on Shannon's face was absolutely incredible, and one I've never forgotten. It was total disappointment, as if she had been shattered. She hopped down and left the living room, dejected and with quiet submission. No one said anything.

What I came to realize from my experiences with Shannon is that at age three she was already experiencing sensory deprivation. She was a beautiful little girl who could verbalize anything. She could tell you all about how this worked and that worked, and what she was doing, and about things in her environment. She had been encouraged to verbally relate to her world, and that's what she was doing.

But Shannon was missing one very important thing for a preschool child, and that important thing was touch. This is why she was so awed when she watched Amanda and me. It was because she had no understanding for the intimacy of our playful touching or for her own ability to experience life through touch.

I have really felt sorry for the experience that Shannon went through and I have often wondered how, in her adult life, she has grown and learned to relate to people.

Balance - it's such a simple, and yet such an elusive concept. How do we stay at a point where we don't exaggerate or negate one or another part of our lives? This book is about balance. It's about relating to the world in ways that include all of the available aspects of life through the entire life span, and beginning in the earliest years. In the early childhood years up to age six or seven, children do not relate to their environment at all the way we do as adults. Parents and preschool teachers often have little understanding of what the child actually needs and very few tools to help them develop in a balanced way.

Development consists of a hierarchy of stages. In other words, each stage of development must have a strong foundation in order for us to proceed to the next. If the base isn't strong, the new stage will not take place effectively. It's like a general taking troops into battle. If there are many losses at the first battle, the troop strength is not enough at the second battle. Each successive outcome is dependent upon what happened before.

A very important law of nature states that, "For every action there is an opposite and equal reaction." I'll refer to that a number of times in this book. To function at your highest mental level, this law of nature requires that you also function at your highest physical level. If you're going to experience dynamic activity, then you've got to have dynamic rest. If you're going to have effective emotional development, you must experience the full continuum from extreme happiness to extreme sadness in your life.

Shannon's world was unbalanced because, with all the value placed on being able to *talk* about her world, Shannon was not being allowed to *experience* her world. I feel that this is the crux of many difficulties that we are experiencing in education today. In Maslow's hierarchy of needs, clothing, shelter, comfort, and security, are basic to our ability to understand and work in the world from a higher level of functioning. There is also a hierarchy of development. Accurate sensory perceptions that tell us about the world must be developed and integrated before we start to use our mental processes to talk about what we are experiencing. If our perceptions are faulty, we are left deprived and unable to fully function.

Learning is finding out what you already know. Doing is demonstrating that you know it. Teaching is reminding others that they know just as well as you. You are all learners, doers, teachers.

Richard Bach
Illusions, p.58

The child is indeed magical, as Joseph Chilton Pierce has acknowledged in his book *The Magical Child*. The process of parenting is also magical, and the process of serving as a resource person to a child's development and growth is magical, too. It's there for our enjoyment, that we should be so lucky to be able to interact with a new life that is full of expectation, full of the joy of all possibilities. I use the words "resource person" rather than "teacher" because I don't believe that adults should consider themselves as teachers for children. If they do, then they should also accept the concept that children are their teachers. But I prefer to think of people acting together for mutual learning experiences.

There's a saying from the East that "The teacher cannot teach, but the student can learn". One of the misconceptions we have in our society is, that we, as adults, must give information to children. For the most part, I think we are proceeding from an erroneous platform. It is true that children need to learn information. So often, though, we present it in ways that are not effective for them, applicable to them, or understandable to them. Simultaneously, because we focus on the belief that children need the content of that information, we fail to see all of the clues that children give us about how they learn. We also don't understand what they could do with that information if we would allow them more space in learning.

The thesis of this book is that things done according to natural law are more fulfilling to us. Children operate very close to the level of natural law, but as a society we succeed in complicating that simplicity to a great degree. Thus, we lose a lot of the basic possibilities that would allow us to live more happy, satisfied, and fulfilled lives.

I feel that this happens because we haven't understood that there is a blueprint for living. This blueprint can be understood from psychological, emotional, spiritual, and physiological positions. If we look to the basis of our existence from all these perspectives, we find common elements.

5

"I...I enjoy speed," Jonathan said, taken aback but proud that the Elder had noticed. "You will begin to touch heaven Jonathan, in the moment that you touch perfect speed. And that isn't flying a thousand miles an hour, or a million, or flying at the speed of light. Because any number is a limit, and perfection doesn't have limits. Perfect speed, my son, is being there."

Richard Bach
Jonathan Livingston Seagull, p. 55

In this book, I will be describing the developmental journey that I believe every human being is intended to make. Then I will discuss some of the tools to help us effectively undertake this developmental journey and tools to use if the developmental journey is interrupted or delayed.

This is not a comprehensive textbook that documents the research on all of the ideas presented. However, resource texts will be identified so that the reader can find the back-up information if they so desire. Neither is the book a collection of information. To touch a person's life to the extent that they will consider change, I both feel and understand that you must also touch their emotional level. Therefore, I have included poetry and prose quotations that give emphasis to what I mean by "living life in fullness."

This is also not a "how-to" book, for I believe that real change involves action. We need both information and experience to fully consummate living in a state of peace and fulfillment, and *you* must have the experience.

However, by providing the information in this book we can help people move through their blueprint for life with the least possible interferences. Most parents would agree they would like to have satisfaction, contentment, security and enjoyment for their children and for themselves.

Development is the interaction of the intent within and the content without. Intent moves the child toward interaction with content out there. The intent within must always be given its content from without. The more extensive and complete the child's interaction with the content of the world out there, the more extensive the resulting structure of knowledge within. The greater that structure, the greater the possibilities for internal feedback, synthesis and volitional control and so the greater the child's ability to interact with more content from without. Through logical feedback, the child eventually develops a volitional control over his own activities and later on in life even volitional control over his own brain activities.

Joseph Chilton Pearce
The Magical Child, p. 13

Chapter 2

The Developmental Highway

My choice of the words "developmental highway" for this chapter title was very deliberate. I considered calling it a "developmental journey," or even a "developmental adventure." However, "developmental journey" infers that we might take some of the byways that parallel or run perpendicular to the highway. "Developmental adventure" implies that there might be a very enjoyable, but circuitous route, at times traveling backward or forward, or side to side. For me the word highway provides the desired image of going the most direct route from one place to another. The highway I am going to consider is the development of our psycho-physiology from conception to death.

As we talk about the developmental process, it is useful to acknowledge that each of you as readers will experience this information from your particular state of awareness, consciousness or stage of development. Those states of awareness or stages of development will somewhat define how you will understand what is being said.

There is an ancient saying that, "Knowledge is structured in consciousness. He whose awareness is not open to the field of unbounded, pure consciousness, what then can words of this structure for him?" This concept implies that we are able to learn from written or spoken words only to the degree that we are able to use our mind and body to understand and feel what is being said. When we think chronologically about the child, the young person, and the adult, we have some understanding that words might contain a different frame of reference for each. But too often we forget that logic, and we act as if everyone is playing the same ball game, so to speak.

Let's take the words "Grandma's house" for instance. If we say the words "Grandma's house," to a four year old child, and the child has not been to Grandma's house, we'll understand that there may not be much meaning associated. In fact, the child's imagination of what Grandma's house is may be something considerably different from what Grandma's house *really* is. If we say "Grandma's house" to an older sibling, who has not only been to Grandma's house, but has spent considerable time there, there is an expansion of this concept. Not only will Grandma's house be understood, but the context in terms of the city and the people in association with Grandma's house will be there. For the parent of that four old, "Grandma's house" may mean the home of their childhood, and the words are associated with a multitude of information and experience.

And so it is when we are reading things out of books and hearing people speak. The words used or the senses that we experience will be in direct relationship with our previous information about that situation. To continue to grow we need experience. Experience along with words can give us fuller understanding.

It is also like this with the idea of stages, or this highway of development. Some of the stages may be very difficult to relate to and understand because they have not become an experiential reality in our lives.

This could be likened to the experiences we have in the dream state, and how different the experiences are from what we have in the waking state. When we try to describe our dream to someone we very often get strong cues that the dream, the way we experienced it, is not at all the way the person that we are talking with *about* the dream is imaging it. So it will be with talking about the stages or pathway points along this developmental highway. Each reader will experience and understand the material from their particular perspective. Hopefully, reading this book will also stretch their knowledge in those areas where they encounter new concepts and information.

Differentiation is the ability to recognize other from self. A summary of the development of our understanding could be that we move from undifferentiation, through all levels of differentiation, to understanding the differentiated in connection with the undifferentiated. In other words, we move from experiencing "everything is me" to cataloging everything that we know in our world, to understanding those cataloged items in the context of the whole. For various reasons that we will discuss later, progress through these stages may be frustrated or delayed. As evidence of this fact, one research project identified that eighty two percent of college seniors still had not accomplished the latter stage of psycho-physical development, which begins at about age thirteen for most of those who do advance.

An additional complicating factor in discussing stages of development is that the stages of our individuality are not one dimensional. We are multi-dimensional beings, although all of the dimensions are interconnected. Any one of these dimensions may be delayed or interrupted. It is very seldom that a person can develop evenly along all stages or dimensions of their existence. To better understand these dimensions we will talk about five different dimensions of our existence - the ego, intuition, intellect, the mind, and the senses.

We can identify the ego as being a very basic component of our individuality. All of the others feed into the ego to give it its own identity - our self concept. Ego gives us our individuality to operate on planet earth.

Next we have intuition, or the understanding and knowledge of natural law. The importance of this level has been greatly diminished in the past century. With the emphasis on scientific methodology, we have not given credibility to this way of understanding the world. And yet, it *is* one way of understanding the world.

Generally, we disregard the input of someone (especially a child) who has knowledge about something, but cannot break down the specific information. Yet, most researchers who have made significant contributions to understanding how the world works (such as laws of physics), have achieved their basic understanding at a time when they were not overtly working with that information. Their work was, of course, well founded in cognitive information, but the actual recognition of new concepts came to them spontaneously. After Sir Isaac Edmonton had proved Einstein's law of relativity correct, Einstein was asked by a student, what if the theory had not been proven right? Einstein replied, "Then I would have pitied the poor Creator. The theory was correct."

Einstein was able to understand that his law was irrefutable at that basic level. There were many other instances where Einstein talked about his understanding being intuitive. He explained how laborious it was to take these whole concepts without words, and begin to elaborate in the linear way required by words to define and explain. The intuitive level, then, is a level of understanding that is very close to natural law.

The purpose of the intellect is to analyze and synthesize. It takes rational and abstract knowledge, and evaluates it for us. The intellect is one of the last aspects of our mind to develop, and the school system is set up to teach on the level of the intellect. It is the rational or logical part of our system. Some have said that it is the intellect that is the basic dividing factor between man and the rest of the animal kingdom.

Next, we have mind, which can be thought of as the integrator of thoughts. Mind takes concrete information from our senses and abstract information from our intuition and puts them together to understand a relationship. Mind is a very broad category, containing both inner and outer aspects of our lives.

Our senses bring us our perceptions of the environment. The senses are our way of relating to everything else around us. An interesting phenomenon to consider is that what we see has two dimensions to it. There is the physical aspect of the way the light rays bounce on the retina of our eyes and on the object that is picked up. Simultaneously, there is the inner dimension of feelings that are associated with that experience. We usually assume that when someone says they see something, they see it the same as we do. If we were able to get inside each other's head and body for a period of time, it's long been my suspicion that we would discover our perceptions differ immensely. It would be as if each of us came from a different planet. Beyond the actual physical act of seeing, the interrelationship of all these aspects of our being would probably give very different perceptions of the world.

There is still one more area that we are a part of but which goes beyond our own personal, psycho-physical existence. We could call it pure consciousness, pure awareness, the unified field, intelligence. Referring to a saying of old, "Knowledge is structured in consciousness." Whatever we call it, it is that which ties everything in the universe together.

Physics, the science of the physical, has long attempted to identify this basic constituent. Physicists began this search with what we see of the universe via our sensory apparatus. They have progressed rapidly as new instruments enhanced their natural senses, to finer and finer dimensions of understanding. At first they saw the grass, then they saw the botany of the grass, (that is the nutrients that were needed and the soil, and the sunshine, and so on). Then they explored the chemistry of the grass down to an atomic level, (the oxygen, the hydrogen, etc.). From that atomic level, they have moved to the sub-atomic level, working with elements so refined they are never seen, but only detected by predicting their behavior. And from that sub-atomic level, those on the leading edge of physics have moved to explore what they define as the unified field. Much progress has been made and much research continues as we attempt to understand what could be identified as the basic constituent of everything.

The eminent physicist, John B. Wheeler, has found, as have so many other physicists, that when we get to these elementary levels, the world looks more like a thought than anything else. We as human beings are physical. At the basis of our existence, we are the same as everything else in physics. Therefore, I am going to use the word "consciousness" as that basic element that ties everything in the universe together. If the reader objects to the word "consciousness," I invite them to substitute any other word that is comfortable. Some would use universal principle, others God, or existence, or wholeness, or intelligence.

From my own intuition, I am certain that in the next years we will identify the unified field that exists in us and exists in every other aspect of creation. I believe there is the possibility that it will be an experiential reality in our lives. The challenge of growing up "inside out" is to gain experiential knowledge of this existence within us while we are busy learning about our physical self in the physical world. As we will explain in the next chapters, this is no small task.

Chapter 3

Creating a Solid Foundation

There is growing evidence to indicate that learning begins in the earliest stages of pre-natal development.

At conception, the new life inherits a particular gene pool from mother and father that is influential in the developing entity through the rest of its existence. Though the gene pool influence has been known for a long time, we have recently begun to examine the profound impact environmental influences have on the developing fetus. We are learning that there is memory throughout the cells of the body. For example, epilepsy researchers discovered that when a muscle is stimulated, in many cases a person may have as much recall of a particular event as if a particular area of the brain were stimulated. Studies also indicate that if a person talks to the baby in the womb, the newborn infant shows signs of recognition of that person. There is also evidence to show that the newborn infant is potentially able to respond to levels of comfort and security to the degree that the mother felt comfortable and secure as the fetus developed.

From conception through the first several months after birth, the infant is in the stage of *sensory motor development*. As the fetus develops and the nerve endings that produce touch, taste, smell, sight, and hearing are formed, information begins to filter into this developing individual and a feedback loop begins. Even in the womb this new existence is, through the faculties of its gene pool and its experience, beginning to learn about its world. This is why it is very important to have raw materials available (i.e. good nutrition and a stable environment) both for the effective formation of individual cells and to allow this entity to grow into its potential.

At some point in the future we may be able to identify more about how the individual's self concept or ego begins to develop

There is an interchange between the individual, the spiritual embryo, and its environment. It is through the environment that the individual is molded and brought to perfection. A child is forced to come to terms with his surroundings and the efforts entailed lead to an integration of his personality.

Maria Montessori
The Secret of Childhood, p. 35

Knowing anxiety to be the great crippler of intelligence, she works purposely for a calm repose. She begins each day in quiet meditation, establishing her union with the flow of life and with her child. She closes each day in the same way and makes her time in between a living meditation, a communion and rapport, a quieting of the mind to tune in on the inner signals. She reduces all the fragmenting intentions of life to the single intent of her act of creation.

Joseph Chilton Pearce
The Magical Child, p. 96

even before birth. While there is evidence that sensory perceptions stored in the brain and body system provide the infant with some significant information about who he/she is within the world, there are also indicators that the world is not seen by the infant as being separate from itself. It seems that there is no differentiation of self from non-self, and that everything is perceived as one at this point in timeless time. In other words, the baby appears to live as if he is the world and the world is him.

To help sort out this complex process of development in the sensory motor stage, I would like to use the work of A. Jean Ayres as she explains it in *Sensory Integration and the Child*. Dr. Ayres, who has been on the faculty of the University of Southern California for more than twenty years, works primarily with children who have learning disabilities. She starts with the belief that before children can achieve intellectual tasks such as reading and math, they must have some very fundamental sensory motor skills in place.

The prerequisites that Ayres considers basic to all others are:

1) the vestibular sense, or the sense of gravity and movement;
2) the proprioceptive sense, or the sense of one's own body parts; and
3) the tactile sense, or the sense of touch. This is how they work and why they are so important.

The *vestibular sense* begins to develop in the womb. Two different mechanisms make up the vestibular sense, both located in the inner ear. The first mechanism consists of microscopic calcium carbonate crystals attached to hair-like neurons. These crystals are constantly pulled down by gravity and shaken around by bone vibration.

The other set of mechanisms consists of three tiny tubes filled with fluid in each inner ear. One pair is up and down, one pair left to right and one pair front to back. The combination of input from these devices tells us whether we are moving or still, how fast we are going and what direction, and where we are in relation to the force of gravity. Through the movement of the mother, the fetus begins to develop experience about where he is in space. After birth, our vestibular senses help us decide if we are right side up, lying down, sitting, etc.

Maturation of vestibular and gravitational senses can be seen readily in the child's growth to crawling and walking. The baby spends time first in a horizontal position (lying down). There is little muscle control or orientation of up, down, or side to side needed. From that age of relative stability, an incredible amount of muscle coordination with neural activity must develop for the child to be able to walk. Just think of all we take for granted to effectively balance while walking on an uneven surface.

Ayres says that gravity is the most constant and universal force in our lives. Development of the sense of gravity orients the individual so that input from the other senses can be sorted in relationship to the individual's own position on the earth. She states, "Vestibular input seems to 'prime' the entire nervous system to function effectively." If this doesn't develop as it should, other sensations will be inconsistent and inaccurate and the nervous system will have trouble "getting started." In fact, the individual will not even gain emotional stability due to this lack of feeling grounded.

The *proprioceptive sense* consists of information caused by the contraction and stretching of muscles and the bending, pulling, and stretching of material between joints. This sense literally lets us know where our body parts are as we move. With a poorly developed proprioceptive sense, a person has difficulty moving around and may appear to be "a klutz," stumbling over curbs and dropping things.

A third basic sense that is developed in the womb is the *tactile sense*, or the sense of touch. Though we often take it for granted, our largest sensory organ is our skin through which we experience direct contact with our environment. Touch is strongly associated with emotions and with social functions. Holding and touching an infant will help her develop and organize the emotional processes of the brain. Touch is critically important.

In *The Magical Child*, Joseph Chilton Pearce talked about the unique bonding that happens when the child makes contact with the mother immediately after birth and hears her heartbeat from outside. It seems the immune system is strengthened. This may be part of the transference that creates wordless memories so richly described by Jean Auel in *Clan of the Cave Bear*.

Some very interesting studies done during World War II showed that many infants in orphanages who were not held or talked to literally died, even though they received their basic needs of food, water, and sanitation. They failed to thrive. It was as if they went into a depression, turned inward rather than moving out into life, and then died.

We also have studies on primates that have shown this same type of result when touch is denied to the infant. One of the conclusions from primate study is that there is a point from which there is no turning back to make changes by simply adding that touch. The primates that were sensory deprived of touch at that early stage did not grow up with appropriate social and sexual behavior patterns.

This research may have immense impact when we understand it in terms of what is going on today in response to problems of abuse and molestation. Because of fear of these behaviors, our society is taking away much of the possibility for tactile satisfaction. Pre-school teachers dare not touch. In an attempt to protect children from abuse, we may be creating a society that is depriving them of tactile stimulation and thereby creating a much greater difficulty down the road. Touch is so necessary at the infant and the early childhood level. We must, under no circumstances, negate this and leave it out if we are going to produce healthy and more fulfilled individuals. Additionally, we must begin to help people learn to touch appropriately. In the experience of many people, touch is either disciplinary or sexual. We all need touch that is pleasant contact to experience our connectedness.

Dr. Ayres mentions that the child who does not establish an appropriate sense of gravity will never become emotionally secure. This seems very realistic because if there is no foundation for movement on earth, the ability to grow fully and appropriately in the next stages of development is seriously limited. It is important we understand vestibular, proprioceptive, and tactile development, so that we can provide movement and touch for infants that will help them successfully achieve these stages.

In the sensory motor stage the child proceeds in a non-differentiated way to move and experience his environment. Perhaps you have noticed that a baby will move arms, legs, the entire body, when he sees something such as a mobile. From the total body movement, he learns progressively to move specific parts of his body. This sensory motor stage incorporates Ayres' sensory integration. The initial way children learn is to experience the world through their senses, and continue to develop until the knowledge of how they can move about in the world is intact.

We, as adults, make a grave error when we believe we can and should relate to the child as we do to other adults. Making the assumption that the child is able to perceive the world in the same intellectual fashion as an adult, shows a lack of awareness of the developmental process. We haven't given the necessary credibility to these developmental stages and the immense role that they play in providing the foundation for what the child will be able to do later on. One of my biggest concerns is that more and more young infants are placed in day care homes and child care centers. Many caretakers in these centers do not understand the importance of sensory integration. Nor do they realize that many repetitions, many opportunities for experience, are necessary for the stabilization of these learning processes.

The next phase of sensory motor development is called motor planning. I have recently been working with a four year old girl who can verbalize very well, but is not able to tell where her body is in space; therefore, she cannot appropriately follow directions such as forward or backward or down. If you mention this to her, there is just a blank look and a switching off, because her mind realizes that she can't do that. I can ask her to point behind her and she can do that, yet if I ask her to walk backwards, she cannot. We're working with her to bring about the integration that is lacking in her development.

Motor planning is a stage that this little girl should be automatically accomplishing. It is a stage in which the child learns how to plan in an automatic way what her body is doing. All of us make millions of motor planning events every day in our lives. Sometimes there are people that you just consider clumsy. Normally, most of us do well, moving about our environment, but then there are days when you are just tripping all over things or breaking things and this is due to lack of good motor planning. For some reason the body is not automatically collating how and where it is moving. Consider the child you were angry with because they spilled their milk or set a toy down so hard it broke. That anger may be very ill placed. Perhaps their motor planning skills weren't developed enough to be able to operate well. We criticize rather than help, and in so doing, send the message that the world is a risky place where we aren't competent.

After sensory motor planning, Ayres talks about the phase of *visual and auditory development*. Again, I really believe that if we were able to get inside another person's head, what we would see or hear would be similar to being on another planet. In the initial stage of auditory development, the child perceives vibration or the movement of the sound waves. It may be more "felt" than "heard." The auditory sense has two aspects -- one is vibration and one is meaning. Initially, the child responds to vibration, and it is by continual repetition of this vibratory quality that the child begins to make associations and pick up actual meanings. What does the child learn if you are continuously angry, nervous, and upset, and yet you keep telling the child, "I love you?" The child must associate the word "love" with those vibratory qualities. Such vibrations are definitely learned at the muscular level and retained throughout life.

The final phase of sensory integration that Ayres talks about is the phase of *lateralization*. In this stage, the new brain, or the neo-cortex, the higher thinking processes that man seems

21

to have, begins to work effectively. There are literally hundreds of thousands of connections between the right side of the brain and the left side of the brain that are called the corpus callosum. These connections initially have to be activated, it seems, by *movement in opposition*. Movement in opposition occurs when the right side of the body, maybe the arm, moves with the left side of the body, perhaps the leg, and those acts of moving the right and the left together activate the process of using the brain as a whole. We come back to the importance of movement, the importance of crawling, and so on, for the child to activate these corpus callosum connections.

Once lateralization takes place, different parts of the brain can specialize. Different parts can be primarily responsible for certain tasks. If this doesn't happen, the right and left sides develop similar functions and this is not very efficient. It requires more concentration, more effort. Specialization allows for the brain to have more ways to function than if both sides had to be involved in the same work. Children (or adults) who have not successfully completed the stage of lateralization may use both hands or either hand for fine motor work, but not well. They may have problems determining right from left. Eye movement across the center line of the body may be jerky, not smooth, creating problems with reading and other activities requiring a flow of vision. We will discuss these problems and some possible solutions later, in the chapter on body movement as a method to enhance learning.

It is most important to understand that these phases Ayres presents are truly developmental in that they build upon each other. Later stages cannot be effectively accomplished until these prerequisites are in place.

Chapter 4

Developing In Stages

Following the sensory/motor stage the child enters the *pre-operational* stage of development. There is considerable overlapping of these stages, and sensory motor skills continue to develop while the child begins tasks in the pre-operational stage.

The sensory motor stage was characterized by non-differentiation (ie., everything was seen as an extension of self.) In the pre-operational stage, there is the beginning of discrimination, a separating out of the person from his world. Now the child begins the process of cataloging. All of us who have known a two year old can understand this. There is an effort to understand differences that often begins with misconceptions.

Piaget, who has done much of the definitive research on the intellectual development of children, shows us how the child at this stage makes errors about "bigger". In his experiments, Piaget took two equal amounts of water and poured one of them into a tall, thin cylinder and one of them into a short, fat cylinder. The child always chose the tall cylinder as being more or as being bigger.

In another case, two balls of clay, equal in size were placed on a scale and shown to balance. Then one ball was made flat. When people in the preoperational stage were asked which was heavier, they said that the ball was now heavier. They believed that changing the shape also changed the weight.

With no backlog of experience for association, light impulses are received by the newborn without recognition. It is the continual input of specific things that allows the child to discriminate and place meaning in their visual ability. Experience continues to be necessary to recognition, even for adults. For example, it is said that when Magellan's ships were out on the ocean, the Indians literally did not see them because they had no thought form for ships, no experience to allow them to see.

Perhaps the reverse of this process is that one Eskimo tribe has approximately thirty-two words for snow. Children in that environment begin at a very early age to identify the kinds of snow using these words.

Discrimination also increases on the auditory level, and it involves the discrimination of sound and of meaning.

The pre-operational stage is the beginning of noticing differences, though the differences are not rationally understood. This transition into the concrete operational stage continues through the elementary years. It is the time when children start cataloging their world. For example, a child learns to connect the word apple with an apple. Next, he learns that an apple is a fruit. Later, the child learns an apple is a fruit and a fruit is a carbohydrate.

Brain lateralization has provided us with two different facilities for learning. One is the discriminative - looking at pieces of the puzzle; the other is the holistic - seeing all the pieces as one. However, we in the West have generally concentrated on discriminative logic, and we have not encouraged people to learn how to put those parts back into the whole. Our school system has encouraged this. In the stage of concrete operations, things are either right or wrong, black or white, good or bad. Laws determine whether our actions are OK or not OK. Tests given in schools have true or false, right or wrong, multiple choice answers, and they do not help children to develop thinking processes that would integrate the pieces into some meaningful whole.

Let's take math, for example. When I say the word "math", many of you probably think, "That sounds hard," because we have consistently put math into the concrete operations of right or wrong. Some interesting studies have shown that if the child is allowed to use both modes of their brain in learning math, they are able to continue to grow and develop and progress in the field of math. One of these projects encouraged creativity. The child was asked "How is it that $1 + 1 + 1 = 4$," and the answers were very ingenious. One of them was that there are three lines in 1 + 1 + 1 and there are three lines in the number 4. Isn't that right? And isn't it interesting that when children were given permission to create, they were able to continue to learn in the field of math?

I feel we have excelled in teaching differences and cataloging. In Piaget's clay ball experiment described earlier, older students will respond that the balls weigh the same because they can put logic above perception. In fact, we now often go overboard in an attempt to put logic above perception in more places than we should. We are taught not to pay attention to our perceptions even when they should have equal value.

Remember the study that found eighty-two percent of graduating college seniors are still in the stage of concrete operations? Rather than having developed to the stage that is called formal operations, those students are still looking at the discrete entities, they are still looking at the right or wrong, they are still looking at things as concrete. *Formal operations* is the first stage which uses the ability to take the parts and put them back into the whole. It is the ability to look at things that have shades of gray. It is the ability to say "Laws are made for the common good and how they apply to me is somewhat of an individual consideration," and make choices around that.

The stage of formal operations is marked by a person's ability to really empathize with another. In the stage of concrete operations there is either this or that, and so the person always perceives things from their own viewpoint. In formal operations, a person has the ability to look at things from the viewpoint of another individual, or even another group of individuals. For example, a person might listen to another and say, "I understand your view. It's one way to look at this. My view is...." And this provides a great deal more flexibility in their life.

Formal operations may begin at around age thirteen. Cataloging will continue, but along with all categories that the person recognizes in life, they will also be able to see the whole picture. Formal operations is a stage that many people never seem to accomplish. This is partially due to our education

25

system, which relies so heavily on concrete operations. Any developmental stage that is not reinforced will atrophy to some degree.

Another factor, no doubt, is the adoration of scientific methodology. Scientific methodology is, theoretically, a great way to understand without our affect or our individual perceptions interfering with the process. In fact, it has been shown that it is impossible for the scientific process to leave out the subjective aspect of experimentation. Even in physics experiments, the observer becomes part of the "field" which affects the behavior or state of that which is observed. And so, if there were no observer, in some senses of the word, the experiment would proceed differently. This goes back to my "Ah ha!" experience, or understanding that scientific research, the method we have held almost sacred for over one hundred years, is basically the product of a developmental stage, or I might say the consciousness, of the researcher. We cannot negate the effect of the totality of knowledge or the totality of development that we bring to any given situation where we are the observer.

At this point I have outlined the stages of development that the Western world has defined. They are stages that have served us well for understanding the continuum of growth with infants, with toddlers, and with adolescents. When we finish with these stages, however, we find that it certainly hasn't explained everything.

Let's return momentarily to the different aspects of the person that we identified as developing parallel and interfacing with each other. These were ego, intuition, mind, senses, and intellect. Here is a summary to pull these relational aspects together.

1. The ego is our self concept, the sum total of our intuition, intellect, mind, and senses. All of those contribute to our self esteem and our self concept.

2. Intuition is the understanding and knowledge of natural law. Within the brain it is more dominant in the abstract area of functioning.

3. Our senses bring us perceptions of our environment. These messages are processed by both our analytical and our abstract brain.

4. Intellect is the discriminator and evaluator of our world. Intellect synthesizes information from the senses and information stored in the abstract and analytical levels of the mind. It is the discriminating factor that sorts through things and decides what we hold as valid. Prior to the development of the intellect, we make "precognitive commitments." These are decisions about how the world operates that are "muscle memory" stored at lower brain levels.

5. Mind is the container of both cognitive and affective information, making it available so that the intellect can do the sorting.

6. We talked about one other aspect that has not been given credibility in our Western science. It is the aspect that I defined as consciousness, or the unified field of physics, from which everything springs.

The focus has primarily been on how we grow to understand and function in the world. We might say it is, "how we know the objective world, the world of objects of which we are one." This certainly is a main task for adulthood. In the West we have seen it as *the* task. Yet, how can we fulfill the Socratic admonition, "Know thyself," if only the external world, the world of things, is validated? From the internal basis of our self (which is that unified field of pure consciousness) through all levels of activity, the full continuum must be a living reality to do that.

In Vedic science, an additional continuum of development is defined. These stages of development are becoming as credible in Western culture as the psycho-physical states we have been discussing. Often called stages of consciousness, and they are indeed developmental stages. They do have a psycho-physical aspect to them, but they deal with both the physical and the non-physical aspects of our being. I will describe the rest of this developmental continuum in Chapter 14, for it applies mainly to the older child and the adult.

Chapter 5

Three Brains In One

A few years ago I came across a theory about the evolution and development of the human brain proposed by Dr. Paul Maclean, Director of the Laboratory of Brain Evolution and Behavior, of the National Institute of Mental Health. Dr. MacLean says that we actually have three brains that perceive and respond to the world in different ways. This *triune brain* can be studied as if it is an archaeological site, with the oldest part of the structure buried deepest.

This oldest layer he compares to the brain of our reptilian ancestors, slightly improved, yet carrying out basic survival functions for our bodies. It is composed of the brain stem, part of the midbrain, and some other structures plus a rudimentary cortex.

Discrimination in the reptilian brain is crude and decisions not very complicated. Danger signals mean fight or flight to the reptilian brain. It manages many "automatic" functions of our body to maintain its physical balance, playing an important role in controlling salinity, sugar levels, body temperature, blood pressure, and the coordinating of more than six hundred muscle structures. It is our oldest evolutionary brain and it is also the first part of the brain to develop in the fetus.

Figure 1 on the following page illustrates, roughly, the parts of the triune brain.

MacLean describes the second layer of brain as the "old mammalian" or limbic system brain, originating in the period when our ancestors were small mammals. They survived by being more alert, more sensitive to their environment, able to apply more diverse responses and be more adaptive to situations. This mid-brain also contains the limbic area which is primarily concerned with our emotions.

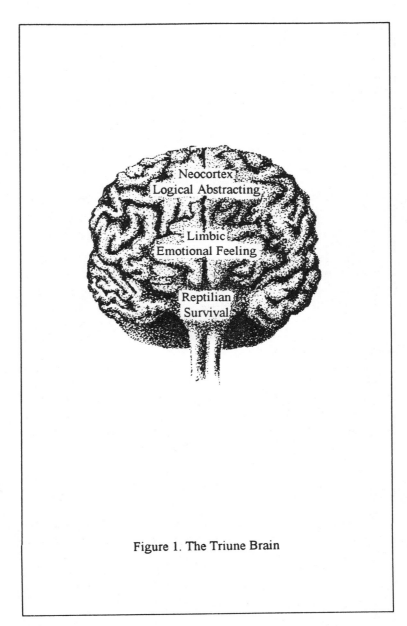

Figure 1. The Triune Brain

The outer layer of the human brain, the "new mammalian" brain or neo-cortex is the largest, most complex structure and the most recently developed. While this is the part we generally think of when we talk about the human brain, it is important to remember that it doesn't exist in isolation. It has its foundation in the reptilian brain and the mammalian brain, and can only function when it is linked with those basic structures.

Through much of pregnancy and infancy, it is the lower part of the brain (the reptilian brain) that is functioning. This survival brain gives the infant an understanding of how to relate to the world. We know that the impulses and the experience that the child has at this point will significantly influence how he relates to his world as an adult. At this time we do not know whether the infant who has a very difficult time surviving because of his physiology or his environment will be affected negatively or positively down the line. For some it seems that it is a positive influence, for others a very debilitating influence.

In times past, theories about infants treated them as a blank slate, tabla rosa, on which the future was to be written. People who have more than one child usually agree that children seem to arrive with agendas already in place. Now, both research and experience agree that when the child's needs are met in the early days, weeks, and months, the child and his nervous system gain a sense of safety, comfort, and trust. This sets a reflexive pattern in the lower, survival brain that is better able to respond and cope.

When a child has to wait and demand to have needs met, the reflexive response sets the nervous system on edge. The child begins to approach his world with more trepidation, less trust and feeling of safety.

Most of what I really need to know about how to live, and what to do and how to be I learned in kindergarten. Wisdom was not at the top of the graduate school mountain but there in the sandbox at nursery school.

These are the things I learned: Share everything. Play fair. Don't hit people. Put things back where you found them. Clean up your own mess. Don't take things that aren't yours. Say you're sorry when you hurt somebody. Wash your hands before you eat. Flush. Warm cookies and milk are good for you. Live a balanced life. Learn some and think some and draw and paint and sing and dance and play and work every day some.

Take a nap every afternoon. When you go out into the world, watch for traffic, hold hands and stick together. Be aware of wonder. Remember the little seed in the plastic cup. The roots go down and the plant goes up and nobody really knows how or why, but we are all like that. Goldfish and hamsters and white mice and even the little seed in the plastic cup--they all die. So do we.

And remember the book about Dick and Jane and the first word you learned, the biggest word of all: <u>LOOK</u>. Everything you need to know is in there somewhere. The Golden Rule and love and basic sanitation. Ecology and politics and sane living.

Think of what a better world it would be if we all--the whole world--had cookies and milk about 3 every afternoon and then lay down with our blankets for a nap. Or if we had a basic policy in our nation and other nations to always put things back where we found them and cleaned up our own messes. And it is still true, no matter how old you are, when you go out into the world, it is best to hold hands and stick together.

Robert Fulghum
All I Ever Really Needed to Know I Learned in
 Kindergarten

32

Chapter 6

Providing the Best Beginning

Imagine the universe beautiful and just and
perfect, the handbook said to me once.
Then be sure of one thing: the Is has
imagined it quite a bit better than you have.

Richard Bach
Illusions, p, 114

This chapter is not so much about doing as it is about being. We have created imbalance by directing our attention on *what to do,* while the element of *how to be* has largely been forgotten. When being is accomplished, doing becomes easy. The ability to be is the basic foundation, the springboard from which everything arises.

We move from being, to intuition, to emotion, to intellect, to action. Or, as Maharishi Mahesh Yogi has said, if we can take a straight course from being to action it results in achievement and fulfillment. Bradshaw says that when we lack congruence this feedback loop is short circuited. Our ability to do continues but it doesn't contain the impact, the energy, the full fabric of emotions, it would if all aspects of ourselves were congruent, moving with direction. We become human doings rather than human beings.

When being and doing exist simultaneously, life becomes a joy. One of the laws of nature we have forgotten, is a law that states, "For every action, there is an equal and opposite reaction." It's interesting how human beings who have the capacity to evaluate and make choices, to be participants on planet earth, choose to overlook the basics.

The laws of nature are very basic to our existence. I emphasize this particular law because when we overlook it, we simply cannot accomplish what we wish to. For instance, if we wish to have dynamic activity, the law requires that we must also have dynamic rest. But we insist that accomplishment takes place only on the level of activity, and we choose to be more and more and more active. Indeed, we get ourselves caught in a frenzy of activities, until the body, as is the case in chronic fatigue syndrome, literally says, "I can't, and I won't do anymore."

If we look around us, we see that nature uses the principle of rest and activity very effectively. If I want to shoot an arrow to the target, I put the arrow on the bow and do what? I pull back. If someone were looking at the logic of this, they might feel that this was in error. I want to get the arrow out there as far as it can go, but what am I doing? I'm pulling back. In fact, when I pull back further, I create greater dynamism to go forward. Pulling back becomes the technique that allows the arrow to go forward. And so it is in most sports. To shoot a basket, you go down before you go up. To swing a golf club, you go back before you go forward.

Contrary to nature, non action does not
mean doing nothing and keeping silent.
Let everything be allowed to do what it
naturally does, so that its nature will be
satisfied.

Chuang-tzu

In our lives we have forgotten this balance. In order to be most effective with children, we must first learn to be with ourselves. If we allow that, we can effectively do and be with them. Unless we continue our own process of unfolding, we do not stay vibrant.

In a conference in Colorado, called *Colorado on the Write Road,* **Dr.** Gabriel Rico, the keynote speaker, talked to educators who were primarily elementary, junior high, and secondary teachers in the field of writing. Dr. Rico told these teachers that if they were not writing, they were doing their students a disservice. Likewise, the primary aspect of successful work with children is to be able to *be* yourself. This is particularly important in early childhood education, for the child at that age relates to his world by how things feel. If *you* don't feel right, if your being is not in order, then what you do with the child will not be congruent on both the being and doing levels.

Infants and toddlers do not initially have meanings for the words you are saying to them. What they do understand or feel is qualitative aspects of the vibration or energy of those words. When you are experiencing an agitated, nervous state within, this will be different from when you are relaxed, comfortable and complete. At the early childhood level, it's very important that adults in the child's life are able to feel a level of security, contentment and comfort themselves. It is this feeling that provides a basis for the child to experience trust in life. Remember, at this stage the child cannot experience himself as "separate from." If he is continuously held by a nervous, uptight person, to a certain degree that feeling of tension becomes his expectation for possibilities. It is very important for you to proceed with your own growth so you can transfer those benefits to the child.

Of course, ideally, the adult also experienced comfort, security, and trust, in their own babyhood. Yet, in our culture it is apparent that this often was not the case. Even though many adults did not have that experience themselves, we must start some place. As a society, we need to settle down, take a deep breath, and enjoy relaxation, in order to promote the well-being of the next generation.

If a significant person in the baby's life has these qualities, it optimizes the possibilities for them to experience the world as a non-threatening place. Their "survival brain" does not become hyperactive and over-responsive to the continual input from the environment. Developing trust at a very early age allows the child to grow and develop throughout his whole life. If he does not develop trust, appropriate development cannot follow. Then stress can automatically cause him to revert to the survival brain and act reflexively according to his initial learning. Therefore, it is very important that these early responses truly help us survive rather than overreact to situations.

Impulses stored in the survival brain (MacLean's reptilian brain) are very basic information that help the infant learn how to stay alive. Although MacLean's three brain systems do interact in many ways, under particular situations of learning, they are somewhat mutually exclusive. When the infant experiences outside impulses paired with underlying feelings of comfort, trust, and contentment, emanating from the adult(s) in his life, he will learn about these new impulses in an appropriate way.

Now, some readers will disagree. They will say that unless there is challenge and stress, adequate learning will not take place. Appropriate information will not be available for a true survival situation. I believe this to be contrary to the evidence.

First, let me give definitions for stress and distress so that we're operating with the same understanding. As I have shown in Figure 3, *stress* is a change from the basic metabolic rate. Everybody operates from a basic metabolic line which varies for different people. This metabolic line is also dynamic, changing continuously for each individual. As we experience input through our senses, it causes change. For instance, impulses coming to the eyes are continuously changing, (tree impulses, road impulses, etc.). Each impulse causes a different stimulation to the eyes that must be interpreted by the brain. The body is set up with an automatic rest phase as stress impacts it. For the eyes, it is the slight blink that gives the eyes some rest. In Figure 2, the line up represents a departure from optimum functioning. The line down returns toward optimum. Illness involves further and further departure from optimum functioning until the body can no longer compensate and death occurs.

Departures from Normal Functioning

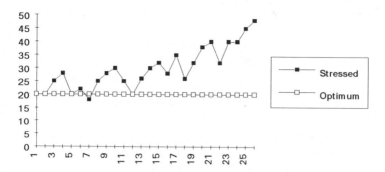

Figure 2. Stress-Induced Departure from Optimum Level of Functioning

Distress is an overload on the machinery of perception. Distress can occur when one sense, or all the senses simultaneously, have so much information coming that it approaches the point of blowing the circuitry. What the body and mind must learn to do is sift and sort the information according to its survival or life protecting mechanisms.

Overload causes chaos within the system and inappropriate learning often takes place during overwhelming events. If the infant has the opportunity to effectively monitor incoming impulses and then respond, there is a higher probability that she/he will be able to respond effectively and appropriately as a child and an adult. When the environment is over-stimulating and/or the significant persons in the infant's life are over-reactive, the infant's body must always do an overwhelming amount of sorting. It strongly incorporates the over-reactive response in order to survive.

Some research shows that when new impulses come in while there is stress on the system, the body changes its biochemistry to create thousands of new neural connections. This means that at the point of *stress* there is learning that takes place and it effectively triggers new interconnections for the brain. However,

37

at the point of *distress* the system goes into such chaos that the new connections, if made at all, may be completely inappropriate. From that time forward, a similar situation will trigger a reaction that is not necessarily appropriate or useful.

For infants and young children, then, it seems that emphasis should be placed on enhancing development through:
- lots of motion and movement
- lots of holding and handling
- a contented and comfortable caretaker.

This will help the child set up effective patterns. When effective patterns are not established, a child may seem to be O.K. as an infant, experience some difficulty as a toddler, and then display learning disabilities as a school age child. Those seeds of disability were there right at the very beginning, but we were not attending to them and allowing for the development needed to overcome them. It's very hard to recognize everything that must be done for the infant, and this is why the adult caretaker must *be*.

A mother's intuition is very credible and it is best accessed from a settled state. From an understanding that is much different than intellectual, the caretaker can often feel what the needs of the child are. When the caretaker operates from a quiet state of awareness, the language of a particular child becomes much more obvious to them.

How is the child attempting to relate to the world? Another premise that I adhere to is that the unfolding of an individual is not a teacher/student relationship. We all participate in a collective way in each other's development. At one time we are the person that provides the model, and at other times we are provided with models. It has very little to do with chronological age. The young child can be a model to us as much as we can be a model to them. It's more of an interplay of unfolding as we work with the child. Understanding her and her needs helps us to understand more about ourselves and our needs.

Recently I had a new "Ah ha!" experience. There is a profound implication in the relationship of children with

The synergetic mode of consciousness operates infrequently but produces exciting results. The development of the previously neglected and undervalued right hemisphere is the catalyst that produces synergetic experiences. Increased traditional formal schooling is not necessarily important in this development. The implication for schools appears to be that nonlinear processes must also be stressed in the curriculum or students must search for them outside the formal school setting.

Michael P. Grady and Emily Luecke
Education and the Brain, p. 39

learning disabilities being in the care of adults who can't be (i.e., adults who have learned dysfunctional rules for living). This implication is that in some children the lack of trust, security, and recognition of their feelings, actually might *cause* the disabilities.

I was working with Susan who had suffered lack of neural muscular coordination (ability to run, perform sports, etc.) as well as learning disabilities (lack of remembering, reading-spelling-math underachievement, etc.). She had worked hard using Domain-Delacato methods, Kephart methods, traditional methods, and she came to me to accomplish more. In working with her I found little evidence of physical inability at this point, yet her language was past oriented, relating her history of problems. In talking with her, I also found out she came from a dysfunctional family system. Suddenly, it struck me that no one had worked with her to establish the idea that she had overcome her disabilities. (This is consistent with the pattern in dysfunctional families that does not support recovery for the "identified patient", since that recovery would threaten all the established interactions.) So, like the obese person who loses weight and then gains it again because she still has a self concept of obesity, Susan was still thinking of herself as a learning disabled person!

I was reminded of Bradshaw's statement, ". . .We programmatically deny children their feelings, especially anger and sexual feelings. Once a person loses contact with his own feelings, he loses contact with his body."

When I realized that shutting down feelings shuts down the body, I actually gasped. Having lost that connection, a necessary link for learning is lost. One sound, profound, reason for learning disabilities is created.

I had known about mind/body connection before, but in twenty years of experience the profoundness and extent of it had never hit me as this did. That night I gave an orientation to Educational Kinesiology[R], a technique to reconnect the mind/body that I will discuss in a later chapter. At the end of the evening a lady asked to talk with me further. In tears, Cindy told me I had just explained her life. She was currently in many different groups, working to correct her problems - over eaters

Where there is a duality, it as it were, there one sees another; there one smells another; there one tastes another... But where everything has become just one's own self, then whereby and whom would one see? Then whereby and whom would one smell? Then whereby and whom would one taste?

Fritjof Capra
The Tao of Physics, p. 128

anonymous, codependency, adult children of alcoholics, developmental optometry, personal counseling, remediallearning. How long will it take us to see the real picture, to treat the whole person? Only then can we be whole and have children who grow into wholeness.

In these early years, we do the infant the greatest service by attending and satisfying all of his needs very quickly so that he learns that the world is a responsive place and that there is not a need to struggle to survive. Until the child actually begins to use the word "I" or "me" or be able to talk in sentences --"I do it," or "Me do it" -- his environment should be structured so that his wants and desires are met as quickly as possible. We want to transfer to the child the information that he is self sufficient and can be satisfied. Since the child does not perceive self and non-self, the responses we give to him are experienced as if he is satisfying himself.

Generally speaking, the idea of punishment for any child under two years old, does nothing but teach the child that there are limitations on himself. This can be effectively learned later when the child can see self and non-self, but not at this particular point in time. The world we set up for the child should be one that is very satisfying and non-struggling. The child that has been hit in early childhood, or continuously has "No," spoken to him at this time, merely learns later on to restrict himself, and to hit (hurt) himself. Restrictions can naturally come when the child can understand them, but there is almost never a situation where a person should have to experience being hit.

You are the bows from which your
children as living arrows are sent forth.
The archer sees the mark upon the
path of the infinite, and He bends you
with His might that His arrows may
go swift and far.
Let your bending in the archer's
hand be for gladness;
For even as He loves the arrow that
flies, so He loves also the bow that is
stable.

Khalil Gibran
The Prophet, p. 18

Chapter 7

Empowering the Young Child

The child eventually shows an understanding of self and non-self by using the terms "I" and "Me" consistently. Now we can acknowledge that the individual ego is intact. At this stage we should begin to work with the child in a mutual relationship. This doesn't happen just over night. Until this time we have intentionally provided everything the child wants and needs to develop their feelings of trust and security. We can't, then, expect them to conform overnight to all the rules of society. But one of the mistakes that we make is not acknowledging that, once ego is intact, the child must begin to develop her relationships with the world and others. It's very important that we help the child from the beginning to know that there is give and take. Our society gives children too many privileges after their ego is intact; we make it difficult for them grow into effective adults.

Let's look at this from a couple of different angles. The child is now operating largely from the emotional mid-brain system. He is still not able to sort out differences logically, reasonably, and rationally, from the intellectual side, but he is getting a sense of these differences. Going back to the law that for every action there is an opposite and equal reaction, life responds to him in the same way he acts in life. I see this amazingly interesting principle working with pre-school children. What they throw out into their environment among the other children, almost immediately comes back to them in kind. Adults have so many overlays that behavior is often not directly reciprocated. But among children, if a child throws out anger, anger will come back to them.

In my pre-school at one time there were two little boys who were very macho. They were always like little roosters trying to attain the highest spot in the pecking order. At the same time, I had a little girl who was very much a princess, very delicate, very deliberate, very cautious in her actions. These two little boys would just be going at it, but when Kimberly approached, their whole demeanor would change almost immediately. One day when we were going outside and down the steps, the boys were jostling back and forth as usual. Then Kimberly came to the steps and, with a split second reflex, one of the boys said, "Kimberly, can I help you?" and the other little boy took her hand. It was so amazing to watch. What Kimberly was putting into the environment was helplessness, and these boys were responding to it by helping. With each other, however, their agenda was to compete for superior placement.

The child needs to learn that what is put out into the environment does come back to them. If the adult caretaker has an ability to interact, rather than just react, the adult will effectively help the child to learn this relational aspect of living. Adults who can most effectively interact are adults who know both the active and the non-active fields of life. They are at a level of awareness where they empathize and help whether there is difficulty or joy. How many parents do we see that are just reacting to their children? Of course, this is one of the causes of abuse. The parent gets lost within herself or himself, and they react in a very inappropriate way.

From age two on, our interactions with the child need to be relational interactions where there are logical consequences. As child psychologist Rudolph Driekurs mentions, the child must begin to understand very early that he responds to the environment and the environment to him. His choices of giving will determine what response the environment will give back to him. There are some delicate situations here. I recall when I was sitting in the airport in India, and a Western family with three beautiful, little blonde children was also there. After a few minutes I realized that everyone in the station was staring at them. They were keeping the whole waiting room in an absolute uproar with their interactions. The children did something and the parents responded "Don't do that," or the children argued between one another and the parents intervened. The contrast

The now inarticulate voice will one day speak, though in what language is yet unknown. This he will learn by paying attention to those about him, imitating the sounds he hears, first syllables and then words, to the best of his ability. Making use of his own will in his contact with his environment, he develops his various faculties and thus becomes in a sense his own creator.

Maria Montessori
The Secrets of Childhood, p. 33

between these interactions and what took place among local families was fascinating. Many Indian families were sitting there, sometimes talking, sometimes not talking. However, they were much more appropriate within the context of the environment. And I got to thinking about the American family and how completely child-centered we have become, probably to the detriment of the child. It seems we spend the early years, until the child is about age thirteen or fourteen, catering to all their needs. Then we wonder why, at age fourteen, they can't function in appropriate ways. Clearly, we have created that situation. In India, the children in those early ages are also very much catered to, but after that they learn about relationships that incorporate the needs of the other children and the adults in that family.

Another of the things we have not incorporated into the family, is the need for parents to grow and progress in their own lives. Among my own peers, those with whom I graduated from high school, many plunged into parenting full force and became superparents. They were often burned out by the time their children were in third or fourth grade. This is too bad, because it is something that need not happen. We have to acknowledge the needs of both the mother and the father. The family shouldn't suffer because everything revolves around the children.

We have accepted the idea that we must constantly entertain our children and this creates one of the imbalances. We believe that, for them to be happy, they must be able to do everything. We have them going to school, and doing gymnastics, and doing dance, and doing music, and doing cub scouts, and doing girl scouts. Their lives are literally scheduled from the time they wake up until the time they go to bed. This is true not only during the school year, but during the summer months, also. It is as if life would be satisfied by doing rather than being.

Going back to the law of equal and opposite reaction, children need to have time to unwind, and it's something we are not giving them. They need time to be.

The studies on infancy show a real need for touch and for sensations that bring about a feeling of warmth and softness and lack of necessity to fight for one's existence. The monkey studies showed that if this is not available, there apparently comes a point where the results are irreversible. When deprived of these sensations, the adult monkey never develops effective social and sexual behavior patterns. Doesn't this say a lot about what we have done in the imbalancing of our society? We have assumed that if the basic needs of food, clothing, and shelter are met, everything will be O.K. We have forgotten about the on-going need to achieve satisfaction through the sensory, and particularly the tactile sense. As I said earlier, I feel that this is critical.

It is my contention that, in ten or fifteen years the generation in their early twenties will explode with rage against rules and regulations that have inhibited them since early childhood. They are inhibited from moving about freely in crowded childcare places and in schools. Parents demand compliant, adult behavior. And children have unmet needs for touching and being touched.

We need to stop treating the symptoms of a few in the society who have not learned to touch appropriately, by saying that touch must be eliminated from the experience of children. If we do not, we risk producing a generation that has no semblance of recognition of the finer values of life.

The difficulty in our society is that we allow the consideration of touch basically in only two ways. Produced over and over again, thousands and thousands of times on the television set and in other media, touch is used as discipline or touch is used with sexual connotations. We do not develop the finer qualities in our own internal lives that allow us to simply touch for health, or touch in the understanding of the connectedness of our existence. Instead, we have created aberrations to touch that never should have been created. When there is denial and sensory deprivation, the need to touch explodes in very inappropriate ways through abusive behavior, either physical or sexual. It is something that we, as a society have created, and it's something that we must take measures to undo.

We need, first, an understanding of the finer values of life that allow touch to be satisfying. I have seen little cards and T-shirts that say, "Have you hugged your kids today?" or "12 Hugs for Good Mental Health, 8 Hugs for Fulfillment, 4 Hugs for Survival." Our society as a whole is reaching out in desperate ways to understand and experience a sense of love and connectedness. We have people in our society such as Leo Bascaglia, who produces a very meaningful platform from which people can make changes just by giving them a sense of love. To some extent we are doing this and dealing with it on the adult level. Yet, we are at the same time negating it on the childhood level.

The schools are a prime area where attitudes about touch must change. But it is not just a matter of allowing and encouraging teachers to touch the children. Educators must, themselves, understand the whole need for appropriate touch, and the learning patterns it enforces.

Chapter 8

Inhibiting Development

Earlier it was stated that stress levels, as monitored by body physiology, were as high for eighty percent of the children in elementary and junior high as they were for top executives. Now let's explore a little bit of what happens under the *distress* response. As you recall, distress is not just a variance from the normal metabolic rate, but is an actual overload response.

Overloads are very individual. They don't have anything to do with how another person may perceive the situation. A particular physiology reacts to incoming information in a way that it believes it must to survive. When a human system perceives a real threat to its existence, the stress response sets up over 200 biochemical reactions within the body. Some of these are quite familiar to most of us. Blood pressure goes up, the heart speeds up, palms become sweaty, there is heavier breathing. These are the external signs. Internally, the digestion begins to convert foods into sugar, which will be needed if the person has to flee or fight. Blood is diverted from the external to the internal parts of the body, decreasing external temperature. This latter change is the principle behind the bio-dot, which gives us one measure of how our body is functioning at any given time. A biodot is a heat-sensitive device that is placed on the hand or foot. As the temperature of the body changes, the dot changes color. Certain colors on the scale show when the blood is moving less into these areas during a stressed state. Under normal conditions, more external blood flow and a higher skin temperature results in a different color of the biodot.

Under stress conditions, it is not a high priority for the immune system to fight invaders. If the body is going to flee or fight, it must be ready for that and not be dealing with its routine activities. So the immune system works much more slowly, if it's working at all. This is one of the reasons that

Among neuron telephones, a stricter propriety is maintained because a single cell may have as many as 10,000 of these direct lines branching out from it, each line in turn branching, linking that cell to anywhere from 30,000 to 600,000 other cells, each with the same paraphernalia. The number of possibilities for relaying sensory information back and forth is infinite; no number system could encompass the possibilities (particularly when we add those 20 million molecules, each capable of producing some 100,000 proteins, within each cell).

Joseph Chilton Pearce
The Magical Child, p. 80

people in on-going stress situations so often get sick. Their immune system is depressed. Also, a person who wishes to lose weight needs to consider their stress levels. Under stress, the body will convert its food into sugars, which disallows for the weight loss process. With the body is distressed believes it needs energy to flee or fight and that energy must come from food. When there is no flight or fight, the body takes the food material not used and stores it as fat. Of course, this is a greatly simplified explanation, but the bottom line is that, to achieve weight loss, you must manage stress.

For our discussion here, the stress response that happens on the level of the brain is the interesting point. At about age seven, this logical abstracting brain should be available for learning. However, every time we undergo the stress response, we automatically shut down that brain system and fall back to the emotional or the survival brain system.

Now it should be clear why we have placed so much emphasis on appropriate early learning. Until age seven, these primitive brain systems are available for learning important responses. But after age seven, we rely heavily on what has already been learned at those levels and respond on the basis of previous learning. When we go into a stress response, the body that has not learned to be over-reactive during those stages when the emotional or the survival brain was dominant, is much more able to make an equitable response. "Here is a stressful situation - this is the way I take care of it - and now I can go on."

However, if the system of the child was bombarded with overload information in those early years, a lot of inappropriate connections were set up. Now the body will respond according to those early interactions. We see this in other people, and we see this in ourselves. Sometimes we react in a way that surprises us, and then afterwards we think, "Did I really do that?" Chances are, it's because of something we learned long ago.

Our ability to be effective adults is the combined response of our experience and these automatic reactions that we have acquired. When we get into survival situations that are very real, very life threatening, we see that people do not all respond in the same way. Rather, they become reactive in the way they previously learned to respond. Individuals in a group of people, all experiencing the same survival situation, have different modes of response. Some modes insure survival and other modes are counter-productive.

Young people need the time to step back and to integrate their experiences. If the young person is stressed much of the time, they are operating from the emotional level. They cannot be receptive to an educational approach based on the logical mind. Yet our schools are set up to educate to the logical mind.

The forgotten element is that effective prior development along the hierarchy described is necessary before intellectual information can be gained. The society as a whole does not allow students to gain the internal values of life in any systematic way. They're learning about the external values of the world. The emotions and intuition must be in balance before they can effectively learn the academic material presented in school.

Under the distress response the child has no recourse but to check out, so to speak, in the learning situation. The distress response precipitates this shut down. It is vitally important that we avoid overloads in childrens' lives. One way we can do this is to give them time to grow within each phase of their development. We need to give what I call assimilation time - time that is not structured, time when they can just be kids. The distress response can result from many different causes, some that we can't control. We can however, allow children time to be children.

Many people are amazed when they come to my pre-school. They can't believe that there are eight children on the premises. I start in the fall with two ideas about the children. One is cooperation, and the other is responsibility. For probably ten years, when children came to me and said, "So and so is doing thus and so," I felt I had to be an intervener and to make the situation right. Then I became aware that children really weren't asking me to intervene. They simply wanted me to know what the situation was, and they were very happy to handle it themselves. I changed my responses to, "Oh, that's interesting. How are you going to cooperate to take care of that?" Or "O.K., it's your responsibility to decide what to do." Then the child or the children were empowered to work with the situation themselves. I have found that they do an absolutely incredible job with things. It gives them the experience of knowing that they have input into their lives.

Most children coming into the school don't have any understanding that this is O.K. They haven't been given the possibility of making decisions and they don't realize they have choices. So from September through January I just keep repeating this concept. From January on, I find I am almost completely a resource person within the context of the pre-school. The children have learned that they can make decisions, and they can carry them out. They can go and be what they want and who they want. Simultaneously, they have responsibility for their actions and for following the few rules that we do have. And they rise to that occasion.

I'm always amazed when I see a child together with parents. Almost immediately the child goes into a manipulating stance that I don't see within the school. They engage in a power struggle. This doesn't happen within the school, and I think it's because I feel they're O.K. My level of expectation is that they can go about and do as they do. But so often the parent-child interaction causes them to be antagonistic with one another. They don't experience this easy flow of interaction that comes about in my pre-school setting.

I've had many people comment, "What is it that you do?" I don't believe it's what I do, but it's who I am and what I allow for the children that effectively lets them grow. While they are in the pre-school, they are in relationship with me, and with others, and with the environment. From that position, there is a very easy response.

Before and after school many children are going into day care centers where the level of excitation is extraordinarily high, just as it is in the school. This is a continuation of stress. If I had my way, I would have all children who need care outside the home before and after school go to a home situation where they would be allowed to be and do. This is the way children functioned in neighborhoods when one parent was not working. The child was at home, choosing their activities and doing as they wished. In fact, I would change all day-care situations so that there would be only a small group of perhaps six or eight children in any one given area. There would be small pod situations where the level of stimulation could be kept at a minimum. High noise levels and a lack of activity overstimulate a human body. Children should be able to move freely and be vocal, but too many bodies doing this will first overstimulate, and then shut down, the child's higher brain system. I don't think that a child under four to five years old should have to be in a homogeneous group of up to twenty children. It is very counter-productive to their nervous system to have to sort all those impulses on a continual basis. It produces an overload and it fatigues the nervous system.

This provides clues as to why children seem to need more and more stimulation as they grow older and may even be one of the reasons why they become involved with alcohol and drugs. The nervous system is subject to fatigue and to notice change there must be more stimulation. Perhaps we can best understand this in terms of olfactory fatigue. When we go into a room where something smells, we notice the odor. But, as we're there for a period of time, the odor becomes non-significant and isn't even noticed. Yet the impulses are continuously being registered for that odor. It's just that our brain has sifted them out. Then a new level of odor comes in and we notice it. The previous impulses are still impacting on the olfactory senses, and we add more to it.

Because they have so much stimulation coming in, and because children are involved in sorting out the elements of their environment as a primary learning situation, they get to a point where they do not notice impulses. They are still being bombarded with them, such as music in the background, but when their system becomes fatigued they need more movement, or more impulses or whatever. Over time this again fatigues the system, more and more is needed, and the system becomes less and less responsive. Moving into alcohol or other substances, can be one way that the child gains more stimulation. The body has lost its sensitivity to a quiet, non-stimulated state.

Through the preschool, elementary and junior high levels, we should give children more time and more responsibility to cooperate with their environment. It is a terrible situation to have parents becoming the busing service for children. Granted, there are dangerous places in the world where parents must protect their children, even themselves. But, when real danger is not a factor, we need to trust and help children to move into their environment more effectively by getting to places on their own and doing things on their own. We have become so protective of young people that we really can't expect them to be effective in their world. Many things are done for them and they are considered the center of all attention.

It might seem a bit of irony at this point, because I'm talking about setting better conditions for children so they can become more fulfilled. At the same time, I'm talking about letting them be on their own more. These really are not contradictory. The developmental stages need to allow them to grow toward the capabilities their society will demand from them later on.

Chapter 9

More Than Curriculum

Because of the way society dictates what the schools can and can't do, any discussion of changes needed in the education system can become a real can of worms. We have a tendency to hold the school system responsible for many of the problems children have. I don't believe the schools are as much at fault as we would like to make them out to be. I do believe that parents and society too often look outside themselves to have things done for them. Too many parents feel that the school is responsible for all that the child is, and will become. They essentially abdicate their own responsibility for allowing the child to unfold who he is.

The other consideration, however, is that we must change from educating only one aspect of life. I think it has been shown in the last several generations, that students just learning facts are not achieving the levels of fulfillment education can and should bring about.

I would like to quote from the beginning of a paper by Paul Gelderlios entitled "Psychological Health and Development of Students at Maharishi University: a Controlled Longitudinal Study." In the introduction he states:

> The purpose of education is to help students grow to become wise, happy, successful individuals and ideal citizens of their country. Educators feel it is their task not only to equip pupils with skills and knowledge, but also to nurture them into mature, responsible individuals who will use their new competencies in an integrated way for the benefit of society.
>
> The conclusion of a recent study conducted by the Carnegie Foundation for the Advancement of Teaching is that present day education does not fulfill this goal. The

studies argue that, "The nation's colleges, driven by careerism and professionalism in education, are more successful in credentialing than in providing a quality education." The students do not develop into thoughtful citizens, but are narrowly trained toward a specialized career. Some of the basic causes indicated by the study are disjointed curriculums whose disciplines have fragmented into smaller and smaller pieces unrelated to the educational whole, and the disagreement and confusion over goals. Bowen notes that the Carnegie report was far from the only one to sound the alarm. For instance, former Secretary of Education, William J. Bennet told Harvard faculty and students in a speech on campus in October 1986, its undergraduate schools, like many others, fail to manifest a clear educational purpose and did not provide a solid moral education.

A widely printed book by University of Chicago professor and philosopher, Alan Bloom, analyzing the present state of education, spoke of the "spiritual malaise" which has led to "impoverished souls" in dazed students. Students lack the capacity to know themselves. Bloom summarizes the thesis in an interview. "The university was founded for freedom of mind, then it forgot what the mind was." The implication is that education provides students with skills and competency, but the students themselves as individuals are hardly cultured in the process.

Paul Gelderlios.
Modern Science and Vedic Science, p. 471-72.

For ourselves and for our students, it's time to consider the growth of both vertical and horizontal knowledge. *Horizontal knowledge* is that which tells us about our world; *vertical knowledge* tells us about ourselves. It's only the combination of those two components that will allow people to become happy, fulfilled, integrated, and satisfied citizens of our country. Without a blueprint of the possibilities of development, we fall

to the whim of whatever is considered important at a particular time.

What we need to do is capture the Fort. By this I mean, if an army wants to control a territory, they have the option of going about capturing the mines, the banks, the industries, etc., or going to the Fort which controls the whole territory. Once they have the Fort, they automatically have all the elements within the territory. In our lives, by moving both vertically and horizontally, we capture the Fort.

In education, one of the first necessary components is that the teachers themselves know how to *be*. It is only from this platform that they can allow the student to be and to do. I'm not going to discuss details of the difficulties within school systems. Most readers will have empathy for this and can go to any of the books listed in the references to learn about specifics. This is about a vision of possibilities that will allow change to happen.

The seeds of successful lives are structured in infancy and early childhood. To develop a quality of life that encourages these skills to mature, seems to take additional input. Traditionally, the family provides role models that allow moral and ethical values to unfold. Yet in today's disjointed society so many families have abdicated responsibility. Children experience a level of confusion through the lack of integrity of the family unit.

Values are learned. If they are not overtly taught, they are covertly learned from the role models available in the child's environment. We have generally assumed these values cannot be taught, or perhaps we have just neglected to accept responsibility for teaching them. Yet, values become the structuring unit for our actions and reactions in life. They are the underlying premise of our lives.

The child who has not effectively bonded with a significant adult, with planet earth, and with society, very often believes that, "Life is out to get you." That's the value that he has learned and the value around which his perceptions of the world are oriented. The child that has bonded with a significant adult,

Your only obligation in any lifetime is to be true to yourself.

Richard Bach
Illusions, p. 125

One is led to a new notion of unbroken wholeness which denies the classical idea of analyzability of the world into separately and independently existing parts....We have reversed the usual classical notion that the independent "elementary parts" of the world are the fundamental reality, and that the various systems are merely particularly contingent forms and arrangements of these parts. Rather, we say that inseparable quantum interconnectedness of the whole universe is the fundamental reality, and that relatively independently behaving parts are merely particular and contingent forms within the whole.

Fritjof Capra
The Tao of Physics, p. 124

with planet earth, and with others in society, feels that the world is a safe place to be, and moves in the world with security. His trust and perceptions and interpretations are based on that.

There have been questions about how these values develop and change, just as we at one time had a question about the possibility of changing or developing the I.Q. We now know that the intelligence quotient can be changed, although it is not generally changed by just presenting more information to a person. The ability to gain information has to do with the openness of the container in which the information is placed. If the container can be expanded, then more information can be incorporated and the I.Q. can be increased. We have found very few techniques in our society that allow this to happen. There are ways, however. For example, scientific research has shown that the practice of Transcendental Meditation (see Chapter 15) can increase intelligence. An ideal school system would be one that was willing to take the challenge and the risk necessary to expand the container for information. An ideal school system would allow the knower to grow along with learning the facts. Psychologists say that we only use ten to fifteen percent of our potential. The reader may want to search for and encourage education that makes the attempt to expand the abilities of the knower as well as teach facts.

It is ironic that we spend so much time in the process of learning about our external world and so little time addressing how that information is understood. In other words, the thought process is the basis of everything that we are, yet we have not looked at where thoughts come from. How do they develop, and how do they move through the intuition, intellect, emotions, and senses? I spent a number of years involved in a research project in the field of consciousness. In fact, I have a master's degree in the field of consciousness. I studied, not what thoughts are, but where they come from. This project explored the basis of being, this pure consciousness, this unified field, as the originator of thoughts.

According to physics, the light impulse is the basic manifestation of all existence. Where does the light impulse come from? Every religion or philosophy has some statement about

The field exists always and everywhere; it can never be removed. It is the carrier of all material phenomena. It is the "void" out of which the proton creates the pi-mesons. Being and fading of particles are merely forms of motion of the field.

Fritjof Capra
The Tao of Physics, p. 208

creation. The most familiar to us is found in the Bible: "In the beginning was the Word." That statement acknowledges the beginning vibration, or the beginning movement that makes up all of creation.

Also in physics, we find the term "virtual photons," which means photons that only exist in potential. They cannot be measured under ordinary circumstances. Then, with some type of stimulated emissions or orderly flow, virtual photons form together to become photons, which manifest in our created world. Everything we see is manifested from virtual photons. In our society, we have given primary credibility to the things that we can see, touch, taste, feel, and smell, and that the scientific community can measure. We have ignored the virtual state that exists before and after it is manifested.

At the age where concrete operations and cataloging take a tremendous amount of time, we must be cognizant that the underlying stage developing allows the child to look at all of the things they have cataloged and perceive the whole. Then they can see the pieces and the whole picture simultaneously. To do this, we must allow the child to speak about his experiences and his understanding, and we must accept the workings of his mind. Rather than feeling we have to make corrections, we must observe and provide our input for further evaluation by the child.

The adolescent years should be the years of putting the pieces into a whole. That means taking the information and seeing how it fits together. A simple example could be apples and oranges are carbohydrates, carbohydrates are the foods that bring energy. Or it could be Denver is a city, in a state, in the United States, on the planet Earth, in the Milky Way, in the universe. This can go to greater and greater abstract levels.

The adolescent must experience action and reaction from the environment. Of course, they still need some protection; they need to live with another concerned, loving, adult. But nevertheless, the child, the young person, should be held accountable to and for her actions and reactions. This will not be so difficult if we have allowed the simultaneous development of the young person within her world. Currently, however, it

"Why, Jon? Why?" his mother asked. "Why is it so hard to be like the rest of the flock, Jon? Why can't you leave low flying to the pelicans, the albatross? Why don't you eat? Son, you're bone and feathers!"

"I don't mind being bone and feathers, Mom. I just want to know what I can do in the air and what I can't, that's all. I just want to know."

Richard Bach
Jonathan Livingston Seagull, p. 14

becomes a time of much confusion. This is because the value system that should be in place for a young person at this point has been overlooked. When the adolescent cannot make decisions based on values we berate her for not being a worthwhile individual.

Destructive criticism should not be used. There is very little information to show that punishment ever produces effective, right, behavior. On the other hand, punishment generally places the individual in a distress situation where they are not able to accurately evaluate a situation, but must simply react to it.

In school systems now, it is generally felt that "time out" is a more effective form of restructuring behavior than anything else. If we think of the way the brain operates, we can see why this is so. When children are punished and placed in a stress situation, they slip into that emotional or survival brain. Therefore, they cannot, on the logical level, evaluate what is happening. That part of the brain is not even functioning effectively. To have a discussion about the event right then doesn't make sense.

However, if the child is removed from the stress situation, they will once again be able to use the logical brain. The body needs a rest phase to mitigate the distress response. When the higher brain processes are again available, it can then process the situation to gain an intellectual understanding of the experience. Destructive criticism, or bombarding the child with negatives about herself, is always debilitating. It is only necessary for the adult to explain their expectations, what is acceptable and what will be needed in the future. The adult should ask for some acknowledgement that the child has heard that information and will attempt to follow it.

It's all so pointless, he thought, deliberately dropping a hard-won anchovy to a hungry old gull chasing him. I could be spending all this time learning to fly. There's so much to learn!

Richard Bach
Jonathan Livingston Seagull, p. 15

In my pre-school one day, I placed a boy in "time out."
Usually, the children are told they can return to the activities
when they feel they can be appropriate. This time, since the
behavior was reoccurring often, I told him I'd return to talk
about it. When I did, I asked him to tell me why I gave him a
time out. He said he didn't know. I asked him to think about it
and said I'd return.

When I went back to him, he attempted to engage me in
another conversation. I asked why I placed him in time out. He
said he couldn't remember. Once again I left and returned,
almost beginning to doubt the tactic I was using. Something
about his response, however, told me he knew and wasn't
saying. This time he said he'd say why when his Mom came.
Though that was forty five minutes away, I agreed and came
back every five minutes. In fifteen minutes, he heard the other
kids going outside and, when I came to him, he told me clearly
and concisely why the time out. The behavior wasn't seen again.
I feel that, until he verbalized it, he didn't own it. Later I saw
the following quote:

> Traditionally, psychologists conceived of thought
> as something that originates inside the individual,
> and only then is expressed socially. Psychologists
> have recently come to realize the great extent to
> which thought emerges as a social process and is
> internalized only after it has been socially
> expressed.
>
> Robert J. Sternberg
> *Teaching Critical Thinking: Eight Easy
> Ways to Fail Before You Begin*

From age thirteen on, education very definitely should
allow for both the subject and the object, or the knower and the
object to be known. I really believe that this lack of affirmation
of the subject encourages alcohol and drug problems through the
loneliness that is felt by the individual.

Recently, I saw an article talking about a highly talented
young lady who recently attempted to commit suicide. The

article blamed the school system for not giving this young person the challenges that she needed. I feel that this is a very erroneous assumption about what could have changed the feelings in that person's life. A person with great talent and ability to gain information in the ways our society presents it, needs developmental balance in the unfolding of other aspects of their life. They don't necessarily need to have more talents explored. Those are going to happen anyway, *if* a healthy balance is achieved.

This article went on to say that the highly talented often don't do their school work because it is too easy. Sometimes they feel uncomfortable because other students are so far behind them and can't understand them or what they are talking about. This is a cop out for our system. The highly talented student needs, as all children need, to grow up with a balanced life; they need rest, activity, physical, mental, social, interpersonal involvement - and to be actualizing Erik Erikson's eight stages of life. With this, they can develop their specialness and enjoy it. We attempt to isolate one part of the person that happens to have excelled developmentally. If we make sure that the balance is there on all levels, that highly talented person can excel while still feeling and being an integral part of society.

This completes the continuum of development as we understand it from birth to adulthood and emphasizes the idea that the person working with the young child is very influential. It also encourages us to allow the young person to unfold rather than attempting to force development based on the surface values of life. This I feel would be a significant contribution to education. Some people may shake their heads and say that it is too simplistic. I would challenge that a longitudinal study should be done, starting with a group of infants and moving through to adulthood. This study should pay attention to the components of balance that deal with rest and activity, of involvement and non-involvement. It should allow for the flow of life, rather than attempt to cram artificial interventions into life. Future generations could benefit greatly from the results of such studies.

We take note of all the details of a disease and yet make no account of the marvels of health. Diseases have been known and treated from earliest times.

Maria Montessori
The Secrets of Childhood, p. 45

Chapter 10

Evaluating Techniques

A myriad of techniques are advertised for the treatment of developmental problems. Some of them are helpful and some are not. Before we go on to discuss techniques that can be implemented if development is interrupted or delayed, I would like to mention some criteria you can use to evaluate techniques.

First, I believe you need to consider whether the process involves both experience and thinking. Is it both passive and active? As we have already discussed, both modes are necessary to incorporate meaning, probably because both the logical and the emotional brain need to participate to achieve full value. Both knowledge and experience have an important part in change.

The second criterion involves a consideration of intuitive and empirical information. From the standpoint of intuition, does the process seem to make sense to you? Do you feel comfortable with it? From where you are beginning, is it something that has possibilities? The empirical part asks, is it credible in terms of testing, or groups of people that have participated? Are participants functioning at a higher level in their own lives?

Both of these points are very delicate, and first I'll address the intuitive aspect. With knowledge structured in consciousness, it's often hard to see what the possibilities are from where we are. This must be why God created parents for children. Babies cannot possibly know dangers, for instance. Children cannot possibly know that varying their situation, going out amongst other people, will give them a broader based experience in life. Their tendency, their inclination, may be to stay with the parent.

You can make sense of the possibilities a program offers only to the degree the levels of your consciousness allow. If we believe the universe is orderly, we can trust that life will take us where we need to go so long as we make the most of our possibilities and be as discerning as we can. This is an important point, because no technique should be thought of as the end point. It only brings possibilities along the way. We need to remain flexible and open, for otherwise we may get lost in the technique and follow away beyond the intended purpose.

Empirical verification also is somewhat problematic. One of my "Ah ha!" experiences was that all of the norms on our psychological tests are based on a population that vacillates around a certain degree of awareness. The person who has gone beyond that in a positive way is just as vulnerable as a person who has gone beyond that in a negative way. We can use research as a guide, but it should never be a final point.

In the field of nutrition, for example, research is very detrimental to a person with specific nutrient needs outside the range of the population as a whole. One of the areas that I find most interesting involves the problem of arthritis. A multitude of nutritional therapies work for individuals, but not everything works for everybody. Therefore, the tendency is just to say that nothing can be done for a person except to resort to aspirin and other medications. I find that, if the person is willing to vary some of the nutrients, it is often possible to bring about complete relief or very much diminish the debilitating effects of arthritis.

At times we have groups of people who are misled because they believe following a particular course will satisfy individual needs and is valuable or vital to life. As an extreme example, consider the Jones incident in Ghiana several years ago. In that situation, a population with specific needs went to their deaths because they believed their ideas were very good and they were being persecuted. If you are evaluating a technique for yourself, you may wish to be discriminating enough not to put yourself in a situation where the risk is greater than the perceived gain.

It is possible to decide that something feels good to you and then find out you sold yourself short. Or, it may seem that substantial research and good results for certain groups exist, and then find that they don't work for you. The bottom line is that we need to consider both internal and external reasons, and then proceed. We take a risk. Perhaps the risk will result in a stress factor that alerts the mind and allows it to make hundreds and thousands of new neural connections. If it does not proceed to a distress factor where the mind literally blows all its circuits and falls back on survival tendencies, we move to new possibilities in life.

In addition, we might also consider where we are at this point in time. Where, in our wildest imagination, do we think we can go? We have the option of just taking in information to learn some things, and therefore we may not need so much of the experiential. If we just want to gain some more information this may be enough. If we want to learn how to do something, it may be O.K. just to memorize that process. However, if we want to move into new meaning, we need to go for both the experience and the knowledge.

As I go through some of the specific ways that it is possible to make change, I want you to know that I am including some of my own feelings and information about a technique. Your process has to start from where you are and where your understanding is.

An important point to acknowledge is that a particular technique may have very little research connected with it but you really feel that it will work, so you do it. And it really does work for you. On the other hand, a technique may have lots of research connected with it, but you don't feel that it's a very comfortable thing. Nevertheless, you say you'll "give it a try," (which even by the statement is acknowledgement of potential failure). And, indeed, it doesn't work. We don't know the mechanics completely, but attitude is a very mobilizing factor in allowing change to happen. We'll go into that a little bit more when I talk about balancing physiological processes.

Let's consider some of the possibilities in the field of psychology for making change. Although there are many new and wonderful techniques now being used in psychology, the primary one in the past was that the person would go to a therapist, and by talking about a situation would gain "insight and understanding". That was the first door of awakening, and yet it seems that if understanding and insight were the total picture, most people in saying that "I want my life to be satisfactory and fulfilled," would have it done. Yet people who have just made a statement about understanding may go out and repeat a situation similar to what they had trouble with in the past. Their response will be as if they had never had that insight or understanding.

In fact, one of the reasons I didn't pursue psychotherapy as a profession was because I felt that it was only working on the symptom level. Dealing with the problem and changing the conditions by talking seemed to be such a long and arduous process that there should be something better. And yet, for a person who was not able to talk about the situations of their life, psychotherapy is a wonderful and magnificent opening. It's just that once that capability exists, we must quickly go beyond it.

We have learned that the emotional brain does not necessarily hear what the person and the therapist are talking about, and this is where change must really take place. So what we really need is a combination of psychotherapy along with experiential processes. Marilyn Ferguson, in her book *The Aquarian Conspiracy*, mentions a list of onset activities to begin to create change in a person's life. Now many psychologists, psychiatrists, and therapists have added new processes that give the person both the experience and the knowledge, and this seems to be a very important factor. Some of these processes are rebirthing, Gestalt therapy, and psychodrama. There's also an emerging area of body/mind therapy. Several of the best known in this area are Rolfing, Feldenkreis, Hankomi,Traeger, T'ai Chi, and Alexander.

One interesting model of how learning actually occurs has been identified and elaborated on at the University of Texas at Austin. It is called the Concern-Based Adaptation Model (CBAM). The premise of the model is that change is available only when there is concern. This concern is not necessarily negative. It's just that there is some impulse to broaden the avenues of awareness. Typical expressions of

STAGES OF CONCERN
TYPICAL EXPRESSIONS OF CONCERN
ABOUT THE INNOVATION

	Stages of Concern	Expressions of Concern
	6 Refocusing	I have some ideas about something that would work even better.
I M P A C T	5 Collaboration	I am concerned about relating what I am doing with what other instructors are doing.
	4 Consequence	How is my use affecting the kids?
T A S K	3 Management	I seem to be spending all my time in getting material ready
S E L F	2 Personal	How will using it affect me?
	1 Informational	I would like to know more about it.
	0 Awareness	I am not concerned about it (the innovation).

CBAM PROJECT
Research and Development Center for Teacher Education
The University of Texas at Austin

concern are shown in the table on page 73. In the CBAM model several stages of implementing or incorporating change are delineated.

The first stage in the CBAM model is the stage of *awareness* about something. You may ask a friend, "What is educational kinesiology?" and they say, "Actually, I don't know what it is." Only five percent of any information that comes into our awareness is ever pursued, but if this person says, "I don't know about educational kinesiology. Where can I get some more information? Is there a book I can read, or is someone going to talk about it?"

The person then proceeds to the second stage, which is gathering *information*. From there, the third stage is *personal*. A person will read about educational kinesiology and decide they would like to learn the technique, and proceed to take a class. The fourth step is *management*. It's here that about eighty percent of people discard what they have learned, because it is at this point of *using* the information that change really has to take place. The person must do something different or proceed in a different way, and this is uncomfortable. According to David Perkins' ideas that once a neurological pattern is set, the tendency is to continue toward our bias. So, eighty percent discard new information and do not experience utilizing it at this point. Is it any wonder that it's difficult to change even when we know intellectually it is good?

The next stage involves *evaluating the consequences*. Has this change helped us or others that we might be working with? Then we make a further decision about whether or not to continue with it. If we continue with it, very soon we will have learned it fully and are ready to go on to the next stage which is called *collaboration*. Now that we've actually learned it, the tendency is to want to work with someone else, see how they use it, how it works for them, and expand on the concept.

Following collaboration, we have a stage that is called *refocusing*. Refocusing means that we're now really in a position to take that information and decide to add new parts to it. We may come up with a new process, or disregard it all together and maybe go on to a new level of awareness. According to CBAM,

this is the process that we go through in life all the time. As you can see, there is much more to learning and changing than gaining information.

Chapter 11

Dynamics for Thinking

How else do we create change and promote balance? How do we intervene so that we become more fulfilled, satisfied, enjoying individuals? One way to do that is to create strong processes the first time. We want to create possibilities for the mind that optimize creativity, focus, and discriminating ability. Some school systems are definitely looking at the thinking process, and within those schools, exciting things are going on. Unfortunately, only a few inroads have been made and these are on the cutting edge. It's not part of the mainstream of teaching. Nevertheless, momentum is building, and it's very encouraging to see. Piaget said that creativity involves the maturation level of the individual, an experience, and socialization. Then everything comes together in what he labeled equilibration. Equilibration could be equated with the "Ah ha!" experience.

David Perkins of Project Zero has said good thinking consists of: 1) the efficiency and precision of the neurological system, 2) content, or knowledge, or factual information, and 3) the organization, or re-organization of thinking. As I expressed earlier, most of the schools will proceed with organization/ reorganization of thinking. However, the efficiency and precision of the neurological system must be addressed at the same time. Irving Seagal has said that once mental structure is there, it doesn't change. He may be right that it hasn't changed very much up to now, but I believe that is because we are not using the technology available to allow that to happen. The technology I have in mind includes nutrition, movement, repatterning, and lack of stress.

Piaget also states that one of the criteria we can use to determine whether or not a student has gained meaning is to ask, "Once the person has achieved a concept, can application be made to a new situation three weeks later?" In order to know whether this is happening, we must focus more on kids and less on the curriculum. Peter Ellsworth and Vincent Sindt feel that in their work over fifteen to twenty years they identified a definite learning cycle. That is, to learn, we start with a question. After the question there is an exploration, a looking at possibilities, a consideration. Then there is an intervention and representation. This primarily means that the exploration is discussed, or the different possibilities are examined. This might include some feedback from the person that is helping to facilitate learning. It has been found that no matter what answer is found, whether it is correct or incorrect, if the student doesn't internalize it, the student will not be able to utilize it about three weeks later.

The application of this process is important, not just in terms of gaining facts or procedures, but especially if we are talking about gaining life skills.

In tests of achievement over the past years, students in the United States do O.K. in the procedure and information aspects of the tests. A lot of teachers and curriculum are teaching to the test, however. In other words, they are giving the information out, the student is memorizing it and regurgitating it. We all know the difficulties with this. The information is not associated with application or meaning. Therefore, it is generally put on the back burner of the brain where it is very hard to access.

David Perkins has talked about three different parts of organizing and re-organizing thinking. The first one he identifies as operations. For example, to analyze a situation perhaps you make a pro and con list about it. The next part of the process is called auto control or meta-cognition. It involves monitoring your own thinking pattern. You may decide, "O.K., I've got to stop and look at the emotional part of this.". And then the third part is establishing cohesive sets of operations. That means recognizing how we can understand or solve the situation. The phrase that Perkins uses here is "what is the onus" or what are the parts in terms of the whole.

On a higher level of thinking such as decision making, you have what is identified as a whole thing process. The goal is to make good decisions. The challenge is to find hidden options, evaluate them, consolidate the evaluations, etc. The parts that make up the decision making have been identified by Perkins as operations, which is the simple thinking processes; looking at the pros and cons; weighting the reason; selecting your best bets; and looking at logical possibilities and consequences.

Another thing that plays into this is attitudes. Emotions here do count as reasons, and one needs to be open minded and proactive. The third part is recognizing signals. Are we vacillating back and forth? Are we feeling stress? Are we enthusiastic? What are the obvious options? Where is the point of no return? When all of these things come together, we sum up and make a decision. I asked David Perkins if he felt that any one of these elements was more important than another. Or were operations, emotions and signals equally important in the decision making process? Since we were discussing this situation from the logical mind, he stated that there really is no one part that takes priority.

My personal understanding is a little different. I believe that the elements of our decision making will be weighted relative to how our needs are being met, and beyond that, how well we learned to satisfy our needs previously. If we feel threatened, if we feel emotional, if we feel stressed, we really will have difficulty looking at the options, both hidden and obvious. Attitudes and perceived signals will take priority unless we are functioning fully physiologically, and unless we have had the best configurations for our prior developmental situations.

We can get some very good insights into thought processes from the assessment that Sindt and Ellsworth have done. First of all, let's consider a problem about pets. Elementary, middle school, and junior high students were given the following problem. Students were given a picture and a story that went along with it. The story was that the students in a school had decided to have a pet fair. One day the students brought their pets, and this is what they had collected (this was shown in the picture.) There were six dogs, one cow, and two cats. The pets were placed inside a fence in the schoolyard and the gates were closed. Someone came along and opened the gate. All the pets ran away. The multiple choice options were: a) did more dogs run away? b) did the same number of dogs and pets run away, or c) did more pets run away? Generally, the answer of the students was that more dogs ran away. They were unable to look at the whole *and* look at the most of the pieces, which in this case happened to be dogs. Again, in concrete operations it is very difficult to look at the whole, or the whole in terms of the parts, or the parts in terms of the whole.

Another situation given to the children involved three separated cubes of one color and five separated cubes of another. The teacher held a bar in front of the students with the three cubes of one color on one end and placed the five cubes of another color on the other end, and the question is asked, "My friend sees things as fractions. What fraction does my friend see? Explain your answer." The majority of answers came back as either 3/5ths or 5/3rds. Do you see why students were responding that way? The answer should have been 3/8ths or 5/8ths, however, these students at the concrete thinking level had no ability to see the parts in relationship to the other parts. This certainly has implications for where we could expect to teach the concept of a particular town being in a particular state, in a particular country, on a particular continent, on a particular world. Generally speaking, about eighty two percent of students on the high school level may not be able to get this concept. If there isn't an understanding of this, how does it impact one's life?

We need to abandon the old assumption that, because we think, we learn. We need to get to the point of looking at where thoughts come from. At present it's an interesting philosophical question, but I predict that in the future it will be identified in our physiology and in the abstract of our existence.

Chapter 12

What You Eat Is What You Are

A number of years ago I heard Maharishi Mahesh Yogi explain a principle of change that has stuck with me. He called this the principle of the third element. His idea was that, in order to understand something, you have to move out of it. For example, if you existed only in darkness, how would you understand full possibilities of darkness. You could look at different shades of darkness, and grope around in darkness, etc., but to understand the full continuum of darkness, you would need the contrast of light. Your understanding is enhanced by something that is different and that comes from an all together new direction. Many of the changes that I'm going to talk about are of that nature. They are principles of the third element, not dealing with the problem on the level of the problem. Often we tend to mull around in all the possibilities of the problem rather than in the possibilities of the solution.

I recently attended a seminar that was very nicely done by David Perkins at the Association of Supervision and Curriculum Development Conference. David Perkins has been the head of Project Zero at Harvard University. Project Zero looked at how we think, and they have made a lot of discoveries. In fact, it is said that we now have about a thousand times more information than we did ten years ago about the brain and thinking. Unfortunately, it has been assumed that we can change thinking by doing different things with thinking. My feeling is that it will only work to the degree that we are able to change or interrupt our previous pattern about thinking.

David Perkins fully acknowledged that we are very lethargic about making changes. In fact, he stated that our thinking about any topic follows our initial bias about the topic. Universally, there is a bias in thinking, (Deepak Chopra calls it precognitive commitment) but people with higher I.Q.'s have

81

more of a bias than people with average or lower I.Q's. That is because they can think about that bias from more angles. It seems to me that our "window of opportunity" is not so much to organize and reorganize thinking as it is to look at the efficiency and precision of the neurological system. We can make some changes there that will make the organization and reorganization of thinking easier.

As a society we tend to deal with symptoms. We tend to address a problem on the surface level of the problem rather than tracing back to the most primary and fundamental reason for the problem. Therefore, I will consider change from several different perspectives. The first one deals with changing the physiological functions of the body. The second one addresses some of the things that are happening to organize and reorganize thinking. Then I will deal with some processes that may address both of these levels, simultaneously. I encourage you to look at the information here and evaluate it. Then look at information you might find elsewhere to expand the possibilities presented here, or even as further possibilities beyond what is presented here.

If we are going to talk about physiological functioning, we cannot escape the reality of the individual's particular genetic pool. The basic factors in physiology are the body's genetic pool and its nutrient needs. Along with this, we must include attitude, exercise, levels of rest, and levels of stress.

According to that law of nature we have been quoting, (for every action, there is an equal and opposite reaction) our body must be in balance to be effective. To be active, it must also gain rest that allows the body to rejuvenate itself. The degree to which the body can do that is also based on laws of nature. Because we human beings have a lot of choices that the rest of the animal kingdom doesn't seem to have, we often decide to break laws of nature and believe we can get away with it. The truth is that we can't. The truth is that the degree to which we act in accordance with these laws of nature determines what we can do and who we are.

Our ability to think depends upon our physiology. We often forget that thinking is not an abstract thing that happens in some vacancy in our mind. It is, rather, biochemical interactions that happen throughout our body. As such, the nature of our thoughts are intricately related to the effective functioning of our physiology. Physiology is the reflector of consciousness. We'll discuss how consciousness affects physiology in a later chapter.

One of the facts of nature is that there are about seventy nutrients that the body needs on a daily basis in a particular balance and proportion. Because we are all individuals, that balance and need varies. We tend to look to others to designate what we need to do. It is good to look at established guidelines, still, we must go beyond those guidelines if we want to individually insure our health.

When we break these laws of nature, the body first tries to compensate, and when it can no longer compensate, it breaks down. The general population almost categorically refuses to see that what we put in our bodies determines what we will achieve in terms of health, longevity and vitality. It is true that the individual's gene pool is also a factor here. But without appropriate consideration of nutrition, we accomplish so much less than we might be able to accomplish.

A quote from the 1987 Journal of the American Medical Association says, "In the coming decade, the most important determinants of health and longevity will basically be the personal choices made by each individual."

As I counsel people concerning their nutritional needs, I am continuously amazed at the gap in thinking concerning food and health. People continue to deny that the quality of nutrients impacts health. There is still a pervasive feeling that illness and disease is something fostered upon us from outside. The medical establishment for the most part perpetuates this despite what I feel is now overwhelming evidence to link diet with health.

I confront the scenario, for instance, of people going on an anti-cancer diet, where the cancer goes into remission - so they go back to the old diet! Somehow they have non-reversible thinking. Food made my body regenerate, but not food can therefore make my body degenerate!

That our ability to think depends upon our physiology has been validated by studies on pregnancy and nutrition. In the animal kingdom we can determine nutrient shortage and birth defects almost on a one to one ratio. Dr. Williams, the Nobel Prize winner, has stated in his book, *Nutrition Against Disease*, in a chapter on "Stillborn, Abortion and Mental Retardation," that, if we paid as much attention to the nutrition of human mothers as we do to animal mothers, abortion, retardation and stillborn infants would largely be a thing of the past. It is very critical that we have the nutrients that our system needs. Because there is disagreement about the amounts of nutrients we actually need, and because eating not only concerns itself with nourishing our body, but also with a variety of emotional and cultural factors, we tend to simply deny the importance of the issue.

We do have studies that have monitored the nutrition of pregnant women and then looked at several factors concerning the infant. They found that women who supplemented their diet and paid attention to nutrition, had an easier time during pregnancy, and during delivery. Their children were ahead in terms of physical development, alertness and mental development in the period at, or shortly after, birth. There also have been studies done with the I.Q. of children showing that nutritional deficits definitely make a difference in mental functioning ability. Unfortunately, we tend to look at this in terms of known deficits. That is, we look at how little we have to have in order to create a deficit, rather than looking at how much we should have in order to create the most effective functioning. We have monitored what *lack* of a nutrient can do to produce ill health, birth defects, etc. We have not shown what high levels of nutrients might do to create optimum health, high physical and mental development, etc.

Nutrients are the basics of every one of our cells, and the law of nature is that those cells must have the right nutrients available to them in order to function effectively. In physics it is stated that systems left to themselves go to greater states of entropy (meaning disorder). We are a system, and entropy occurs if the system is left to itself. We have to incorporate orderliness from the environment. That is, our body must convert foods into primary components that it can use to keep it functioning effectively. We can illustrate this by picturing a Volkswagen that has been set out in a field. If nothing is done to it, it will begin to break down, rust, etc. Of course, the environment that it is in also determines how much that is going to happen, but it will eventually break down without care. The same thing happens with our physiology.

Dr. Edith Weir, the Assistant Director of Human Research for the United States Department of Agriculture, stated a number of years ago that if even the minimum daily requirements were eaten by the public, over 200,000 deaths a year from cardio-vascular disease, and over 100,000 deaths from cancer would be prevented. This is how critical the necessary nutrient levels are to us. To allow yourself and the children with whom you interact to function more fully as individuals, I very much encourage you to take a close look at nutrition. Follow the dietary guidelines on a daily basis. Be concerned and know that you can take care of your own health to a great degree. You can be responsible for being in tune with your body and following through with the signals that your body is giving you. Stop poisoning your cells with non essential non nutrients such as sugar, additives, artificial concoctions.

Now, how do you get in tune with your body? One thing you can do is to stop buying into the idea that you naturally have some aches and pains. Naturally, the state of wellness is a body that has an absence of aches and pains. That body is vital, energetic and enlivened and can carry out the activity of the day. When this doesn't happen, you need to look at the signals that your body is sending you. We have been taught to overlook those signals. We have been taught that, if we have a headache, take an aspirin -- if we are constipated, take a laxative -- if we have indigestion, take an antacid. But the headache and constipation

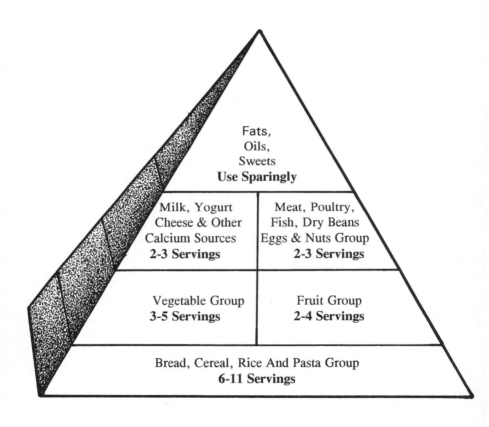

Figure 3. Dietary Pyramid

and indigestion are the body's signals. They are signals that ask you to pay attention to what is going on. Tune in to the body, so that you know what these symptoms tell you about the body. If you are aware, you can then take a look at the possibilities for change.

If you don't have a health professional (a person that is well versed in holistic health) to consult with, you can go to a book called *The Nutritional Almanac*, that contains a wealth of information. Here you can begin to get an idea of what those nutrient sources are and what they will do for you, as well as to look for what nutrients might be needed when your body gives those signals.

Now, obviously, if you have a very acute pain in your right side, you don't look at this book and attempt to correct it. You go to a physician or a surgeon. For emergency medical care, there is absolutely no substitute. But, if the problem is something that you recognize as sort of on-going, you can give yourself a week, two weeks, three weeks (because most of us have already given ourselves a year, or two or three years with these symptoms). And you can begin to alter some of the variables for nutrition. I can practically guarantee that if you begin to do this and attend to balance and not to extremes, there will be an improvement in your health, generally in four to six weeks.

Let's look at the dietary pyramid on the previous page. Did you plan, prepare, and eat according to this guide today? What about yesterday? What about your family? This pyramid gives the necessary foods and quantities that give coverage for the "average" person. This does not include those a) under stress, b) with infections, c) with allergies, d) smokers, e) with weight considerations, f) on exercise programs (you get the idea). For all of these situations, the body needs more or different combinations of nutrients. *Yet, to start thinking in relation to this pyramid is essential.*

I find that women often have a big protein deficit. Protein is a builder of cells, and if the body does not have enough protein, then the cells cannot do their work. Approximately forty five grams of protein is the suggested intake per day. Particularly if they don't eat breakfast, women generally get thirty to forty grams of protein. This may not be as true for children, for the average man, or in a family that is still eating a meat and potatoes diet (though that diet will pose different problems). In my own life, I have found getting enough protein can translate to needing one to two hours less sleep daily.

Do you get at least two cups of vegetables a day, one of which is dark green or yellow? Do you get six to eleven servings of grains a day? Do you know what grains are? This will just barely cover your B complex needs. B complex helps the nervous system do a number of things -- one of which is thinking. If you don't get this, I highly recommend that you supplement. As a matter of fact, my background in nutrition and evaluating diets of hundreds of people tells me that almost no one is willing to take the time to plan, prepare, and carry out the dietary guidelines every day of the year. If you don't, you simply put your health in jeopardy.

All foods are not equal. We were taught to believe that if we drink a glass of orange juice (made from concentrate), eat an orange picked off the tree eight weeks ago and shipped to the grocery store, or eat an orange that is ripe and fresh from the tree, those forms all contain equal nutrients. It has been shown that two trees in adjacent orchards may vary as much as 200% in their vitamin C content. So, it is true that not all oranges are equal.

And then there is a new paradigm to consider in relationship to food - the effect of the theoretical field theory.

In classical physics, which was the pinnacle of understanding until the 1920's, the world perception was that the universe was made up of matter and energy. Matter was concrete. That is, a tree, a person, a rock were separate and solid and were ever that way. Energy (e.g., electricity) was moving and stayed in that form. With the publication of Einstein's theory of relativity, the perception of the world according to physics changed dramatically.

With this new understanding, matter and energy were interchangeable. Not only that, but everything in creation existed relative to the field it was in. Field theory showed that everything exists in relation to everything else, and therefore is influenced and changed by everything else. Unfortunately for us, food science and medical science stayed in the classical theory model. Rather than changing their perceptions to match that model, nutrition and medical science held that if two people ingest a food or a medicine, it will be same for both of them. Nothing is further from the truth!

An orange or a medicine in your body and mine are very different because the field that is your body and the field that is my body are very different. The ramifications of this are awesome. The food industry has been allowed to create altered, synthesized foods that bear no relation in our body to the foods of nature. Hasn't anyone noticed that there is a parallel rise in processing of food and declining of health?

Looking at what western science has contributed, we have a starting point. Eating according to the food pyramid would vastly improve our health. But we must discriminate more, so that the foods are not so processed and adulterated. We need to go even further.

Now that I have negated the status quo, what do I have to offer as an alternative? A form of balancing the body with foods to create health does not even need to be invented. It comes to us from ancient times and is known as Ayurveda or "science of life." You may have read Dr. Deepak Chopra's books. Dr. Chopra very profoundly and eloquently gives the science and metascience that underlies this knowledge.

Very briefly, Ayurveda teaches that the body and all of nature as well as the seasons are made of primary elements combined in different ways that give rise to different forms. The elements are earth, water, fire, air and space. Our bodies are dominated to different degrees and from different needs for balance at different times of year. A person who has more water and earth elements will look physically different from a person with more air and space elements. If the water, earth person eats lots of food dominated by water and earth (such as dairy foods, beans, breads) and does this in spring when water element dominates the season, they may experience an imbalance due to too much emphasis on these elements. A common imbalance at this time is allergies and mucous.

This system considers the person in relation to the illness or disease and attempts to recreate balance that disallows dis-ease. The western system looks at an illness as being the same for all persons, rather than the illness in relationship to the individual. For an indepth presentation of Ayurvedic health, I refer you to Dr. Chopra's books: *Quantum Healing; Perfect Health; Unconditional Life;* and *Ageless Body, Timeless Mind.*

In the bibliography I have referenced several books that can shed light on the idea of changing thought processes through nutrition. Basically, we aren't just affecting processes, we are affecting general, over-all health.

The child that comes to school in the morning after eating a donut and a can of pop is not exactly a candidate for mastery of the mind. They might be able to function on that diet for some period of time, but the potential that they are losing is very, very significant. We need to understand that by eighteen months, all of the brain cells that we are going to have, we have. Yet the brain continues to expand. This expansion can be accounted for by the development of new neural connections. These neural connections must be made of protein, vitamins, and minerals, and they use carbohydrates as their fuel source. So it's vitally important we address nutrients when we're considering both the thinking process and making changes. Some studies show that children who eat a healthy breakfast, generally attain higher grades in the morning.

The body cannot live without being fueled, anymore than an engine can fly without being fueled. I think of some children that I have worked with in the field of nutrition. One pre-school mom who came to me with a three year old and a three month old said, "I'm going nuts. It seems like a conspiracy. One hour Tim is awake, the other Andy is awake." I suggested that they increase both calcium and protein, and it worked, as it has in probably a hundred other cases with which I have worked. These two little boys happen to have inherited a genetic sensitivity to sugar and tend to be hypoglycemic. When the blood sugar dropped at night, it triggered an adrenalin response, which then triggered something similar to a nightmare, and that awakened the child. Protein held the blood sugar level higher longer. Calcium provided the nutrients that are termed "the lullaby minerals" because they have a settling effect on the nervous system. There are many other examples that I could recall, particularly in the realm of working with children with allergies, but it has been very much my experience that good nutrition can allow change to happen and allow improvement in the thinking process.

Chapter 13

Learning Through Movement

Educational Kinesiology ® was chosen by the National Learning Foundation as one of a few innovative techniques available for education. Educational kinesiology was created by Dr. Paul Dennison, who had a remedial reading center in California. He was, himself, learning disabled and kept pondering the difficulty of making changes in learning through remedial techniques normally used. He felt that practice simply enhanced the problems.

When a child has difficulty with a concept or a procedure such as reading, we naturally assume that more experience with reading will make him a better reader. But what if he is not reading correctly in the first place? What if the way his eyes move, or the way his brain is processing information, is not appropriate in the first place? What does practicing that inappropriate procedure do? Generally, it does not improve the skill of reading.

It is unfortunate that this point is so seldom understood in the schools. In fact, when I teach Educational Kinesiology techniques, I find that the most difficult group to reach is teachers who work with learning disabled kids. I think it's safe to say that most teachers come out of college with a process firmly in mind and are ready to change the lives of children. However, when they get into the techniques, and into the processes, they find that change doesn't happen very quickly.

Over time they begin to see that these techniques accomplish very little. Instead of being hopeful, they become very hopeless, and the children feel this. When a teacher feels hopeless, children feel that they are not able to learn. They see that what they are doing is not improving their skills, and instead of becoming empowered, they become incapable.

Dr. Dennison became familiar with a physiological process that is used in the field of health, a muscle tone bio-feedback mechanism that gives signals about how the body is functioning. This process is based in the ancient Chinese system of healing with acupressure and acupuncture. Rather than focus on the solidity of the body (such as the blood, etc.) these processes work with more subtle influences such as the nervous system. The nervous system operates on something very much like electrical currents. These electrical currents are a type of energy that influences the physical body. In many cases, when changes are made at this level, changes occur easily in the mind and body.

Many of us are familiar with the concept that change can be implemented by working with the energy fields within the system, rather than on the physical level. Dr. Dennison wondered if Touch for Health, which was created by Dr. John Thie, could be used for working with children who have learning disabilities. He wondered if we could signal to the body via muscle tone bio-feedback to make changes on the level of the mind, and he began working with this idea. He found that muscle tone bio-feedback was seemingly a language that the body could understand. This is more fully elaborated in Barbara Meister Vitale's book, *Unicorns Are Real: a right brained approach to learning*. Here, we are not working with the logical abstracting processes that are accountable for only one part of our existence, but with the muscle memory or the pre-cognitive memory, memory that is probably stored somewhere in the survival or emotional portions of our brain. In working with muscle tone bio-feedback and Educational Kinesiology, I have found that muscle tone is the way that the body, or the precognitive function, is able to orient to change and allow it to happen.

Since Dr. Dennison's initial finding in the remedial field, people who use the technology of Educational Kinesiology have found that it is applicable not only to remedial learning, (which presents the extreme condition for application) but for average and above average students. It seems to lessen distress response in learning, and allow for new levels of neuro-muscular integration in athletes. For adults seeking personal or professional change, it seems to be a process whereby the body can be retrained or repatterned out of the old habits. They can then do what they intellectually understand they need to do. For the elderly, Educational Kinesiology can create a continuing balance in brain integration so that both hemispheres of the brain work together more effectively. It works to the degree that the body and mind are willing to reorient.

Rather than focusing on the symptoms, a practitioner of Educational Kinesiology works to isolate and change some fundamental actions based on experience and understanding of old belief systems that are no longer relevant. For instance, rather than using more reading to help a person read better, it concentrates on where the body is not cooperating to allow for reading (the eye muscles, perhaps). For the person who wants to lose weight, it might focus on how a person's life would be different if they didn't have that weight. Then the process would set up in the neural structure the possibilities of the body allowing that to happen. There may have previously been some mis-learning that has not allowed the person to fully cooperate in the process. Maybe that person doesn't feel they deserve to lose weight, or maybe they are afraid of their sexuality and what responses they would elicit if they did lose weight. There are any number of issues that could be addressed rather than just the issue.

A fascinating consideration here is that the body doesn't have a reality of its own. It proceeds "as if" what it *thinks* is true. For instance, the person tends to perceive a smell "as if" this situation of smelling were similar to previous situations of smelling the same odor. If a person has happy thoughts, the body responds bio-chemically in a favorable manner. If the thoughts are sad, then quickly the body also responds "as if." The most definitive elaboration of this, of course, is in Norman Cousin's book, *The Anatomy of an Illness*, where he talks about the role of laughter in curing serious illness.

Well, then, we still ask the question, "Do thoughts come from the outside or the inside?" The trigger point may be external, perceptual information, but what the body does with the perceptual information involves the internal mechanisms of understanding. The Educational Kinesiology process looks at how the *body* is understanding a situation.

Now, when we talk about something, we tap into the logical brain. Talking is something that this higher brain can understand. But when we use muscle tone feedback we are tapping into the emotional or survival brain system.

Let's walk through this process again to show how it works. Remember that in the developmental process up to age seven or so, learning is done primarily with the survival or emotional brain. We also have some understanding that about eighty percent of everything we will ever know except factual information, is learned before age seven. If the body perceives stress or distress, it physically begins to mobilize about two hundred different metabolic processes. On the level of the mind it shuts down the logical abstracting functions, because they aren't necessarily a priority at this time. If the body experiences distress, its priority is to flee or fight in order that it might survive.

We have an interesting drama building here. When we learn on the logical brain level and do not have a distress response, we can very fluidly move from that logical brain and into the emotional brain, back and forth, to create what we need. However, under the *distress* response, (a stress presents an alert to the body, and a distress presents an alert and survival response) we don't have those higher thinking capabilities fully available.

How much information did we have as three year olds, or as five year olds, to create appropriate action and reaction in difficult situations? We didn't have nearly the range of experiences, of course, that we do now. However, the effectiveness and efficiency of those actions determined the ways we learned to survive and utilize information. And if our body was always in overload, then the effectiveness and efficiency is highly questionable. Now we get to our adult years and the body experiences distress. Our logical brain shuts down because we're going to survive; we move to take the action that was learned in the same or similar situations back at those early levels of experience. Is it any wonder that we have difficulty?

If we have a way of working with the pre-cognitive emotional brain the way words talk to the logical brain, do we not set up the possibilities of achieving a great deal more than just working from the level of intellect? My experience has been that this is, indeed, what seems to happen. When we utilize the body to make change and cooperate with the mind to make change we have something that is much longer lasting.

I'll relate a recent experience I had with Jason. He came to me as a second grader, hating school, hating reading, very negative toward cooperating, feeling that things were being done *to* him. I did an initial evaluation, and I could see that his eyes were not moving effectively from right to left and left to right. When they got to the middle, it seemed that there was a turning off and refocusing, and his eyes jumped every time. So I explained to him that his eyes weren't working very well, and they weren't cooperating. It was no wonder that reading was so hard and it wasn't much fun. I also explained that, although he really liked sports and was doing a good job, if his eyes would cooperate, he would probably do even better with sports. But it was his choice whether to work on it or not.

Of course, when a child perceives that they haven't had any choice, and they can now make a choice, they generally go back to the pre-operational developmental stage that says, "No." And that was Jason's response. I left it at that, explaining to him that no one could make him do anything. After all, they hadn't been able to make him read yet. In a few days I got word from his mother that Jason would be willing to work with me. So he came over and we went through the process that is called Dennison laterality repatterning. Also, we used Brain Gyms^R which are some simple exercises to help us learn through movement and signal to our body to integrate our brain. Justin did better on his before and after check for reading, and definitely better on tracking with his eyes after the repatterning than before.

In Educational Kinesiology we use muscle tone to signal the body. It is tested by simply putting the arm out at a right angle to the body, suggesting a specific situation, and then putting a slight pressure on the arm. This is not a strength test, but just

The integrated mode of consciousness, by using both hemispheres jointly, will exhibit traits of unity, syntheses, and balance. Inappropriate, fragmented approaches to problems will be replaced by those that are holistic, but will include linear approaches that have prevailed until recently. The integrated mode of consciousness will not only provide new solutions, but will apply the balanced approach to problems that was previously lacking.

Michael P. Grady and Emily Luecke
Education and the Brain, p. 37

pressure that allows a trained person to evaluate whether the body is cooperating with the process or not.

After working with Jason, I took him outside to run a timed sprint. I had him look once at parallel lines on a piece of paper, and run the sprint. Then I had him look at an X on a piece of paper and run the sprint. His time improved after looking at the X. A little later, his three younger brothers and sisters, his mother and myself were out at the sandbox. That piece of paper with the X and the parallel lines had fallen down. I was talking to his mother, not paying attention to Jason. Jason picked up the paper and asked his mother, "If I put my arms crossed out in front of me, could you lift me up?"

She said, "I don't know."

He said, "Well, do it."

She gave it a try but was only able to move him about a half inch off the ground. I still didn't understand what was going on, but then Jason asked his mom, "Now do it."

She reached down to pick him up and, much to her surprise, lifted him about a foot very easily. Jason's response to her was, "I was looking at the X and thinking heavy the first time."

In his own mind he had incorporated fully the concept of integration and had come up with this example of how it could work for him. Many children have no lack of intelligence. They only have a lack of accessing it so it is used effectively.

Because children are so much more affiliated with the emotional aspects of their existence, this is a process that they can buy into. It is one that they will rally around to make change, even when all of our intellectual processes don't make much of an impact.

We need to reiterate that it is not thinking that allows change to happen with Educational Kinesiology, although cooperation probably helps to facilitate the process. I worked with a little boy who is autistic, and I could not even get him to do a number of the processes, but his mother could do them or do them with him. I was working with him several thousand miles from my home, and after only an hour and a half of instruction, I returned home with the promise from his mother that I would hear from her.

I didn't for a very long time. Then one day I got a request in the mail for several of Dr. Dennison's *Brain Gym* books. She explained that, since I had worked with Mark, he had begun to communicate a lot more. In fact, he now was able to be understood by members of his family and his improvement was noted enough in school that they were willing to take a look at this simple process.

The reason that this process is often overlooked is that it *is* simple, and we don't have a history of results to look back on. We work very concertedly with children, doing physical therapy and occupational therapy when there is an obvious disability. Why is it that these same procedures have not enhanced the lives of the so-called average and above average person?

I have had many other positive experiences with Educational Kinesiology, and the feedback I receive is that the process works because it interfaces with some of the primary interruptions in learning. It begins at the level of development that has been interrupted or delayed. It also empowers children, because they can see it is something they can do and they can see the change that occurs.

Working with adults is another story. In order for Educational Kinesiology to be most effective, the adult has to be in a cooperative mode. Before we reach adulthood, we have become well attuned to the idea that people do things to us, not that we cooperate with them or can facilitate the change ourselves. So adults come in to work with Educational Kinesiology and want the trainer to make the change for them. We work only as facilitators to identify where change needs to be made and then facilitate the process through the muscle tone bio-feedback.

If the adult feels that we are going to do something *to* them, or if they choose to say, (because they were dragged in by a spouse or whatever) "This isn't going to work," - chances are, it won't. For it to work, there must be an allowing participant. People who are kinesthetically, or touch oriented, seem to have

From birth, the growth of intelligence is a progression from the concrete toward the abstract. By concrete, I mean the physical substance of the living earth (its rocks, trees, people, winds) and its principles (such as fall down, go boom, and fire means burn). By abstract I mean the products of the mind-brain's own creativity.

Joseph Chilton Pearce
The Magical Child, p. 14

an easier time with this, but with cooperation, it can work very nicely for anyone.

Negative, inhibited patterns and negative compulsive behavior patterns can become an impediment to making change. In these situations, it may be necessary to first deal with problems that originated in childhood by attending workshops on healing the wounded child within. Muscle tone biofeedback allows us to make change from the level where the difficulty occurred. I've worked with adults, for instance, on telephone call reluctance with sales people. They know that in order to make the sale, they have to make the call, but they can't because they have had some negative experiences of people not being kind to them. That becomes an overriding factor, even when it is something that determines whether or not they are going to be successful.

I have also worked with people who have allergies. Many people love their allergies. It's the only way that the body has found to get the person to take care of themselves. It's too bad that it has to be done in an uncomfortable situation like that. In fact, I posed the situation to one lady whose allergies began in earnest after the birth of her first child, and then really compounded after the birth of her second child. I had some information that suggested the problem. Now that she was responsible for these little beings, who was going to take care of *her*? Her body set up this configuration to insure that she would be taken care of. Never mind all the discomfort that goes along with that. It was insuring it's survival, or insuring that she would be taken care of.

I also worked with a seventy eight year old lady who had learned that she could only feel good when she was sick. Her mother had been very abusive to her, and her memory was that only when she was sick was her mother kind. So if someone was kind to her, she got sick, and if someone was unkind, she got sick. Both ways reinforced the idea of sickness and kindness.

In a sense, what we do with Educational Kinesiology is rewrite the adult's history at a neural and muscular level. We send signals to let the body and mind know it's O.K. to make change. Before that, once something was marked indelibly on the lower brain, it was retained in spite of all the intellectual activity. Now we can signal that it's O.K. for change to occur.

Educational Kinesiology can be a vehicle for changing habit patterns to alleviate feelings of abandonment, to be able to express one's self, to express care and love, to be able to do the activities necessary for success in one's profession.

Use Educational Kinesiology to play sports better, to have a better golf game, for instance. An athletic trainer told me that, once a person had learned a sport, he could coach them to correct what they had been doing ineffectively. While he was there, they could do it right. However, under the pressures of tournament competition, there was about a ninety nine percent probability that they would revert to their old mechanisms. We need to signal the body that it's O.K. to make changes in a way it understands, and the body will respond even when the coach isn't around.

In the process of aging, brain cells die, but new neural connections can often still be made. I feel the integrating activities can, in some cases, be useful in slowing down the aging process.

With the elderly, I have found that doing the simple Brain Gym exercises allows more flexibility of their minds. A recent experience was with a lady with Alzheimer's who had given up social engagements, and was having difficulty doing the simple things that she needed to take care of herself. We used repatterning and the Brain Gym exercises to give flexibility to the body and to signal the brain to work in an integrated way. Within a short period she was taking much more responsibility for her own care. She even went out to tea, and carried on a conversation with another person.

For some time we have understood the role that mind plays in creating effective body responses. Olympic athletes use visualization and mind processes to allow the body to perform better. We have taken no effective look at what role the body plays in allowing the mind to function more effectively.

Good research by Westinghouse Learning Corporation identifies a correspondence between motor performance and mental functioning. And yet, what are the first things that go when we are experiencing difficulty with the school budget? It is often our exercise program. Again, we look to the symptoms and try to make change from that level rather than looking at probable causes and initiating change that is far-reaching.

Educational Kinesiology is a process that makes change by impacting both body and mind, a process that should be considered by all educational systems, by all therapists, by all people who are working in the motivational field, as well as those who are working with the elderly. The technology is only limited by the creativity of the individual who is using it. It works to create change for specific functions.

Chapter 14

New States of Awareness

In beginning this chapter, I need to clarify semantics. In the following sections, I have used the term "state of awareness" in an attempt to distinguish the difference between "state of consciousness" and "stage of consciousness." In both Maharishi's writing and Alexander and Langer's writing, "state of awareness" and "state of consciousness" are used interchangeably. The important point is that a *state* is defined as "the condition of a person or thing with respect to circumstances, qualities, etc." States of awareness or states of consciousness include waking, sleeping, and dreaming. A *stage* is defined as "a single period or phase in a process of development."

We have emphasized appropriate physical and neural development (or objective knowledge) in discussing the psycho-physical developmental stages. Currently, learning who the person is that knows (subjective knowledge) is not a part of our education even though it is the basis for everything we know. While gaining knowledge about the world, we must begin to gain knowledge about our essence, our self. The full experience of this comes as we develop beyond formal operations. In his excellent book, *Unconditional Life*, Dr. Deepak Chopra writes:

> The opposite of self-referral is object-referral, which means giving primary importance to externals instead of to myself. A person whose thinking is based on object-referral automatically assumes that his mind has no influence over things in the outside world. A thought is a subjective event that ricochets around inside a mental bubble, never able to break out. For all practical purposes, this means that object-referral

awareness is mercilessly dominated by things. Compared to the ghost of a thought, the hard, solid objects of this world seem much more real and therefore much more powerful. This is the position almost all of us find oursleves in.

While it is common in our culture to place credence in objectivity and declare it more trustworthy than subjectivity, it can be treacherous to rely psychologically upon exterior objects. To illustrate the changeable quality of objective reality, Dr. Chopra recounts the following fable:

There was a poor villager who had only two things of value--his son, and a handsome gray pony--and he loved them both dearly. One day the pony disappeared, and after searching unsuccessfully, the villager became deeply dejected. Three days later the pony returned in the company of a beautiful black stallion. The villager was overjoyed. He hugged the pony and immediately claimed the stallion as his own.

His son was eager to ride the wild horse and begged his father until the father gave in. But the stallion was too spirited for the boy and threw him off. The boy's leg was shattered, and he had to be carried home on a litter in great pain. The father's joy turned to sorrow.

As the villager sat in front of his hut, weeping and wailing, a company of soldier's rode by. They were preparing for war, and they came to the village to drag off all the eligible young men as conscripts. When they saw that the villager's son was injured, however, they left him at home. Once more, the father's sorrow turned to joy and he delighted in the tragedy he had mourned the moment before.

"In real life," Chopra says, "people have more than two things they cherish, but the result is the same. So long as our happiness depends upon objects 'out there,' we are their prisoner. We have given our freedom away to things."

The following quote is by Maharishi Mahesh Yogi, the founder of Transcendental Meditation, who observes:

If we look into the process of gaining knowledge, we find there are two sides of knowledge. The object of knowledge, which we seek to know, and the subject of knowledge, the knower. What the present system of education provides for is knowledge of the object. What it misses is knowledge of the subject - knowledge of the knower, in its infinite capacity. When the knower is ignorant about himself, the whole structure of knowledge is baseless.

Jn. of Modern Science and Vedic Science,
p. 472 quoted from American Association
for Ideal Education, 1985, p. 5

The continued development of consciousness allows us to begin to understand the external world as it relates to the unified field. To be able to do that, we must first have the *experience* of that unified field. Throughout the ages, intuitively it seems, humans have wanted to understand this connectedness and this integration. We have used many terms to express the possibility of moving into this field of integration. People are intrigued on the intuitive level by the thought of moving that direction. Those who have the best facility for allowing this to happen are people who have completed the development of the stage of formal operations, since that is the platform for further development. However, it's also true that people move through these stages at different rates. Someone at a lesser stage of development may acquire the impetus or the inclination to move quickly on to further stages of development. Vedic psychology, an ancient body of knowledge, adds further understanding to the

developmental highway and unfolds the tenets for living life in fulfillment. In the book, *Higher Stages of Human Development,* **Alexander and Langer (1990) wrote:**

> Vedic psychology has a decidedly developmental orientation. It delineates seven major states of consciousness (Maharishi, 1972). The daily cycle of waking, dreaming, and sleeping constitute the three ordinary changing states of consciousness. In addition, Vedic psychology describes an invariant sequence of three stable higher states of consciousness based upon experience of a purely nonconceptual fourth state of consciousness. Our life-span model proposes that these stable higher states constitute "postconceptual" higher stages of development that are consonant with, and dramatically extend, the Western "organismic model" of ontogenesis (Overton & Reese, 1973).
>
> It is typically held that transcendental experience is transitory and accessed by only a privileged few....In contrast, based upon Vedic pshcyology, we propose that these higher stages of consciousness naturally unfold in the course of "normal" adult development but that development "freezes" prematurely because of accumulation of stress and lack of exposure to appropriate environmental support or developmental technologies. Thus, we suggest that to label such higher stages as "mystical" is a misnomer, for they "transcend" the representational domain in no more mystical a way than abstract thinking transcends the sensorimotor (or preoperational) activities of early chidhood.

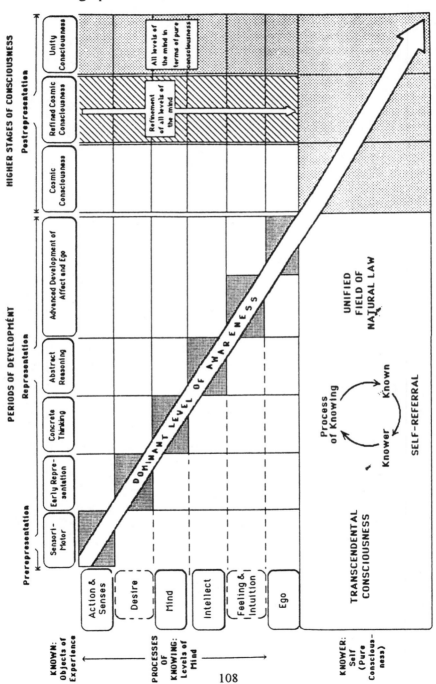

In the Figure on the previous page, from Alexander and Langer's book, the levels of mind are represented, from gross to subtle, down the left side of the chart, while the general periods of development are listed across the top. The authors state:

According to our model, when awareness shifts to functioning primarily through a deeper mental level, this newly activated process of knowing is increasingly differentiated from the more expressed levels of thought and action and becomes the dominant locus of functional awareness. For example, when conscious awareness comes to function through the intellect in a reflective manner it provides the foundation for abstract reasoning such as formal operations....The reflective intellect, which involves the capacity to think about thinking, now represents the primary locus of conscious awareness. All the levels of the mind less subtle than the intellect are differentiated (solid lines separate the levels) and their contents can be taken as objects of knowing. Although their influence may be substantial, all levels of mind more suble or abstract than the intellect remain relatively undifferentiated and less available to conscious utilization and control (a dotted line separates these levels). However, because the levels of the mind constitute the inherent structure of consciousness, they all are to some extent active at all times and each contributes to every thought and partially undergirds every cognitive phase. (This is why...all the levels of mind are represented or contained in each column of cognitive development.) (p. 294)

As I have emphasized in previous chapters, growth and development requires a combination of experience and information. People need both experience and knowledge to understand the external world completely and the internal world completely. How does one experience the totality of consciousness? This has been a very elusive and very mystical area of pursuit throughout the centuries. It seems that people have not been able to do this in a systematic way at any time or age. And, it's also quite probable that the way to allow this experience may be somewhat individualized for people. If, by happenstance, you get the right person with the right process, there are results. Yet, there seems a high probability that the force of nature to experience itself is strong. It seems unfortunate that people need to go through so much trial and error. People who experience another level of consciousness for themselves often try to give the experience to someone else, but it doesn't seem to happen effectively. These other stages of consciousness are not attained through cognitive or experiential understanding. It is identified by Alexander and Langer as a post-language, post-representational stage. To make matters worse, when attempting to understand this stage, they go on to say:

> According to Vedic psychology, all the periods of development described would fall within the range of the ordinary waking....In contrast, higher stages of consciousness are said to be as qualitatively distinct from ordinary adult waking (and from each other) as waking is from the states of dreaming and deep sleep. On the one hand, we will see that development of these higher stages appears to involve the natural continuation of unfoldment of deeper mental structures. On the other hand, the higher stages can be viewed as dramatically, "discontinuous" with (i.e., highly distinct from) prior periods of development (p. 308).

We know the later stages of child and adolescent development must follow the development of sensorimotor skills. These later stages move beyond the sensorimotor stage and encompass and use the sensorimotor skills. So too, the higher stages of consciousness move beyond earlier stages of development and require the use of skills acquired in those earlier stages.

Here, we encounter a methodological problem How do we describe stages that are indescribable? Formal operations is the highest delineation of consciousness the West has to offer. Dr Deepak Chopra, in his book *Unconditional Life*, does a great job of explaining step by step how we structure our reality. Dr. Chopra exposes the possibility we could break with those investments that keep us from living our lives in freedom Beyond that, readers may gain appreciation for these stages because they are inherent to our developmental process. In fact, some people may be living these stages without being aware of it. All they experience is that their world seems to be different than that of most people. If the stages are natural, then we don't have to try to develop them.we need only to allow them to unfold. Nevertheless, fullness is complete through knowing. If you don't know you have diamonds, you may not feel rich. Knowing validates experience.

Just as we can use appropriate processes to advance earlier stages of development, certain techniques do initiate new stages of consciousness and a different style of functioning of the nervous system. The one with which I am most familiar is Transcendental Meditation ® (TM). From more than three hundred fifty scientific experiments in countries throughout the world and over the last thirty years, TM has consistently brought about changes on a physiological level and a psychological level.

It was shown in the late 1950's by Dr. Robert Keith Wallace that we can identify different states of functioning in the mind and body by measuring physiological parameters. We can identify through measurements of a person's physiological conditions when they are awake, when they are asleep, and when they are dreaming. Using these measurements of physiological conditions, Wallace compared the state of subjects in these three natural states with those practicing TM. He found that during the process of TM there was another psycho-physiological state that could be measured. This was characterized as restful alertness. The physiology during this state received extraordinary amounts of rest as measured by oxygen

111

consumption, even compared to sleep. At the same time, the mind maintained an alertness.

Wallace found that even the brain wave configurations during this period of time were different than those that the person experienced during the waking state. This state was identified as a fourth state of awareness called *transcendental consciousness* and it has, through many further experiments, been identified as a state of pure consciousness. This is analogous to a person, within their own ego and physiology, who is able to experience the unified field of existence that the ancients talked about in terms of integration and fulfillment. This is a state rather than a stage of development. Again, we quote Alexander and Langer (1990, p. 309):

> Maharishi...states that awareness becomes completely "self-referral" when "consciousness has nothing other than itself in its structure..." He further explains: "Consciousness in its pure state, fully open to itself alone, experiences itself as this self-interacting reality of nature...consciousness knows itself to be the knower, the known, and the process of gaining knowledge--all three values simultaneously in one....In this experience, the divided state of the bounded self is transcended and the one unified Self is experienced as I-ness, amness, or Being, unqualified and unchanged by active states of becoming, such as thought and feeling..." Maharishi further describes Being in the language of the Vedic tradition: "Experience shows that Being is...*Sat-Chit-Ananda*. It is *Sat* that which never changes; it is *Chit,* that which is consciousness; it is *Ananda*, that which is bliss...Being is the basis of life, that which gives it meaning and makes it fruitful..."
>
> ...Transcendental consciousness is a fourth major state, as opposed to a stable *stage* of development, which can be temporarily experienced either alone (as doing TM) or along

with the active levels of mind and changing states of consciousness....Only when this silent, self-sufficient state is *permanently* maintained along with waking, dreaming, and sleeping, does the first stable higher stage of consciousness dawn. Thus during any developmental period, when awareness momentarily settles down to its least excited state, pure consciousness can be experienced. Nevertheless, in the absence of a systematic technology (such as TM) to culture this experience, those few individuals who frequently have experienced pure consciousness are already likely to function habitually at a subtle level of mind, in close "proximity" to the Self (1990, p. 309-310).

When this "silent, self-sufficient state is permanently maintained" the higher stage of consciousness experienced is called Cosmic Consciousness.

One of the things happening here is a refinement in perception. In this fourth state of awareness, we have begun to do a perceptual figure/ground shift. We explain that in terms of the first four stages of psycho-physical development, in which the objects of the senses, the *things* in our world, have been the primary object of what we understood about our world. Everyplace, we saw things and identified things.

In experiencing the fourth state of awareness, we allowed the mind to resort to the other end of its continuum. It recognized the basic level of that which did not contain things, but just was. From moving into the world and experiencing the physical world in which all the things were seen, we move to the non-thing stage.

Another way to look at this, is to say that when we are in a room, we, by habit, are used to looking at the things in the room--the chairs, and the cupboards, and everything. But if we do a perceptual switch of awareness, we can see that there is actually more space in the room than there are objects. Our habit of perception has not allowed us to look at the space. We've concentrated on the things.

Likewise, when talking or reading, the only way that words can be understood, is because of the space between them. And yet, we do not notice the space. We have been in the habit of looking at the words.

Familiarity with the fourth state of awareness allows us to make this perceptual shift. Things that have been on the foreground move to the far background, and the space, bliss, unified field, pure consciousness, that has been in the background now comes to the foreground.

Mental energy is consumed in great amounts when the mind keeps on thinking and wandering. Every thought, in order to be a thought, consumes quite a lot of mental energy. If thoughts arise one after another, mental energy is being consumed all the time; if fewer thoughts come, less mental energy is consumed. If the mind is established in bliss consciousness, it remains contented in itself and does not wander here and there thinking useless thoughts.

Maharishi Mahesh Yogi
The Science of Being and the Art of Living,
p. 161

Chapter 15

Completing the Blueprint

The stage of Cosmic Consciousness often happens intermittently for a period of time before becoming integrated. The next state of awareness described in Vedic literature talks about experiencing the integration and connectedness of the fourth state simultaneously while going about in the world. They describe a state of awareness that maintains the full continuum from that restful alertness or silent level through the levels of activity. The characterization of this state of awareness is that the mind and body function on the experiential and cognitive level of life, while at the same time, the broader awareness of the unified field, pure awareness, or unboundedness, is maintained. The nervous system simultaneously maintains two styles of functioning--boundaries and unboundedness.

This expansion of consciousness could be likened to the broadened perspective of a parent compared to the child. Let's say that the child is on the floor playing with his truck, and just having a great time zooming around. The parent is sitting on the couch, watching the child and enjoying the fun the child is having. This continues until, suddenly, the truck bumps into the coffee table and a wheel falls off. The child becomes absolutely distraught. He feels the whole world has been destroyed, nothing is going to be the same again, and there is much anxiety. The parent, with a broader awareness, is able to comfort the child and enjoy being able to do that. The parent is not dumped down into this isolated situation, and realizes that it is a transitory one.

The next morning the parent gets ready to go to work and drives onto the freeway. He or she is traveling along, and low and behold, a wheel falls off the car. How does the parent respond at this point? Is the parent now in the situation that the child was in, when it seemed that his whole world was destroyed? Or is the parent able to maintain a perspective of the whole? Can the parent see everything in relationship through their broadened awareness as they did with the child's situation? The fifth state of awareness could be likened to this. It's the capability to move through life without being caught in the isolated situations of life.

From Alexander and Langer (1990):

> The unbounded Self, in cosmic consciousness, is classically described as "non-attached," not in the sense of being withdrawn, but because it is no longer identified with or overshadowed by the boundaries of the changing values of thought, perception, and action..., much as the concrete operational knower no longer shares the narrow attachment of a five-year-old to a single salient aspect of the stimulus array on conservation tasks (p. 314).

They go on to state:

> When even the finest level of mind is completely transcended, consciousness assumes a unified field character allowing direct Self awareness. Thus, the primary constraint of the prior representational periods is overcome in that the question, 'Who am I?' has been fully resolved. Self knowledge may now be said to be direct and complete. Knower, known, and process of knowing are unified in the unbroken, self-referral experience of pure consciousness. In terms of our life-span model, this process of differentiation of the Self culminates in what could be termed *subject permanence*--stable experience of the nonchanging Self as opposed to changing representations of the bounded self. From our perspective, this developmental milestone is even more significant than the emergence of object permanence during the transition from the

prerepresentational level. This permanence of Self constitutes a radically new level of invariance providing a completely stable, expanded inner frame of reference (p.314).

"After some time of alternating the fourth state [transcendental consciousness] with the other three, the nervous system becomes habituated to maintaining that state of [pure] awareness...Then that state of awareness is maintained even during waking, dreaming, and sleeping. All the jerks and jolts of activity during waking, the rest of the night, or the delusive nature of dreams, all this is not able to overthrow the reality of the fourth; it is forever maintained (Maharishi, 1972)." (p.315).

The integration of advanced states of awareness into the stage of Refined Cosmic Consciousness was described in Alexander and Langer by an advanced female meditator as follows:

The experience of [pure] bliss consciousness has become more clear, intense, and stable not only during meditation but also during activity. Now I find that a soft but strong feeling of blissful evenness is present most of the time...This evenness is so deep and stable that it is able to maintain its status even in the face of great activity. Even when faced with great problems, this...evenness cushions one against all possible disruptions and makes all activity easy and enjoyable...somehow my responsibilities seem to arrange themselves so that they can be accomplished with very little doing. In this way activity has become more and more effortless while leading to greater accomplishment. (p. 317)

Without a concrete experience of this, one of the ideas that might come to mind is, "Well if that happened, life would just

become 'blah'." The reality is that this is one of the greater states of freedom and one of the greater states of enjoyment. Who needs to be overwhelmed by situations? To enjoy the continuum of life, and to be able to move in it as one would like to, expands one's possibilities immensely.

How many people have had the experience of saying, "I just lost myself in that situation." And what a feeling of being out of control! In this fifth state of awareness, the control is there, but it is not the individual's ego control. It is the control of flowing within the laws of life. Because it does not break laws of the natural world, of their own individual psycho-physical existence, individuals in this state are able to have spontaneous right action. This means they are able to move through life doing the best possible thing for themselves and for others.

This fifth state of awareness would seem to be fulfilled in itself, yet the Vedic text continues that this only serves as the platform for the next state of awareness to develop. With the fifth state of awareness the individual has been able to understand his own individual connectedness to the whole, the unified field, pure consciousness. This gives a great deal of satisfaction. However, once that is incorporated, it seems there is the possibility for the individual to experience not only his own individuality in terms of the whole, but the connectedness of other things in terms of the whole.

To allow this to happen, there needs to be a refinement of the senses, because it is through the senses that we are able to identify everything in our world. Through most of our developmental stages we have seen things as self and non-self. We have identified non-self by experiencing the world through our senses. Refinement of our senses expands our perceptual base. Then we are able to sense in everything else that same basic unified field as we were able to see in ourself.

It is analogous to a description that Maharishi Mahesh Yogi has often used. He says that there is a colorless sap that moves through the tree, and the gardener who is able to tune in with the tree will be able to understand the colorless sap as the basis of the tree. If there is something wrong with the tree, the

118

gardener will not go out and tend to the leaves and the branches and the bark, but will go to the source of the tree, the colorless sap. When that gardener identifies within himself the basis of pure consciousness, then he can identify the colorless sap within the tree, and will know that it is the same basis that was found within himself.

In the final state of awareness there is movement so that things and space (the unified field) occupy equally, so that they are simultaneously available. The space, or pure consciousness, that is a part of one's own individual aspect and the space that is a part of all of other things, is now experienced. In this sixth state of awareness we are able to look at something else and see that the basis of one's own individuality and every other individuality has the same component. Alexander and Langer (1990) state:

Similarly, according to Vedic psychology, although the knower is perceived as particulate and clearly separate from the localized objects known on the ordinary thinking level of mind, when all the faculties function from the subtlest possible level mind, then a corresponding level of maximum refinement is appreciated in objective creation as well and the rigid boundaries dividing subject and object begin to dissolve...(p.319)

Maharishi describes this growth of unrestricted love and appreciation: "In this state of [cosmic] consciousness, the Self is experienced as separate from activity. This state of life in perfect non-attachment is based on bliss consciousness, by virtue of which the qualities of the heart have gained their most complete development. Universal love then dominates the heart....The heart in its state of eternal contentment begins to move, and this begins to draw everything together and eliminate the gulf of separation between the Self and activity." (p.320).

**This refinement in perception of objects was experienced by
English poet, Kathleen Raine, and Alexander and Langer
(p. 322) quote her lovely description:**

> There was also a hyacinth growing in an amethyst
> glass; I was sitting alone....All was stilled. I was
> looking at the hyacinth, and as I gazed at the form
> of its petals and the strength of their curve as they
> open and curl back to reveal the mysterious
> flower-centers with their anthers and eye-like
> hearts, abruptly I found that I was no longer
> looking *at* it, but *was* it; a distinct, indescribable,
> but in no way vague, still less emotional, shift of
> consciousness into the plant itself....I dared
> scarcely to breathe, held in a kind of fine attention
> in which I could sense the very flow of life in the
> cells. I was not perceiving the flower but living it. I
> was aware of the life of the plant as a slow flow
> or circulation of a vital current of liquid light of the
> utmost purity. I could apprehend as a simple
> essence formal structure and dynamic process.
> This dynamic form was, as it seemed, of a
> spiritual not a material order; or of a finer matter,
> or of a matter itself perceived as spirit. There was
> nothing emotional about this experience, which
> was on the contrary, an almost mathematical
> apprehension of a complex and organized whole,
> apprehended *as* a *whole*. This whole was living;
> and as such inspired a sense of immaculate
> holiness. Living form--that is how I can best name
> the essence or soul of the plant. By "living" I do
> not mean that which distinguishes animal from
> plant or plant from mineral, but rather a quality
> possessed by all these in their different degrees.
> Either everything is, in this sense, living, or
> nothing is; this negation being the view to which
> materialism continually tends; for lack, as I now

knew, of the immediate apprehension of life, as life.

From this platform, still another stage develops to give completion to the experience in life of moving from non-differentiated through all different levels of differentiation and back to non-differentiation. This Unity Consciousness is a continuing refinement of perception such that we are able to experience individuality and unity of everything simultaneously.

It might be likened to going to a play. When we are at the play, we have an awareness of where we are, and in addition are able to associate to a degree with all of the different characters that are playing on the stage. On one level we know that we are not the play, and at another level we allow ourselves to be a participant in the play. Throughout their lives, most people get stuck, thinking they are the actor on the stage and not being able to see the broad perspective. Because they can't see the broad perspective, they aren't able to play their part nearly so well.

If we are able to see the internal and external part of the world as both the observer and the participant, our life can be more full because we have a broader perspective. Following that, we might be able to look even further and identify that a part of every character is in us and we in them, as well as being able to maintain perspective.

Again, Alexander and Langer (p. 323):

> At this level, even the process of experiencing the world is said to become fully self-referral: All levels of mind and objective reality are experienced in terms of the Self. "...in that state, the ultimate value of the object, infinite and unmanifest, is made lively when the conscious mind, being lively in the unbounded value of awareness, falls on the object. The object is cognized in terms of the pure subjective value of unbounded, unmanifest awareness....In this unified state of consciousness, the experiencer and the object of experience have both been brought to the same level of infinite value, and this encompasses the

entire phenomenon of perception and action as
well. The gulf between the knower and the object
of his knowing has been bridged....In this state,
the full value of knowledge has been gained, and
we can finally speak of complete knowledge
(Maharishi, 1972, lesson 23, p.9)".

Now the stages of development have been completed, and it
is a miracle, indeed. I am sure that the reader can anticipate
challenges along the way that interrupt or delay the
developmental process. And yet another perceptual change needs
to take place, for what we have done in our world is to adore
and exonerate the difficulties as if they were necessary, and get
caught in them. Rather, we should perceive life as a process
which has its natural beginning, middle, and end, and yet from
another perspective is not a process at all, because it is all there
simultaneously. All we have to do is to allow it to unfold. If we
expect that to happen, we can truly bring about the adage that,
"Where we put our attention, that will grow stronger in our
life."

It has been found in research that the attention factor, the
attitudinal factors, all have a great impact. In fact, Brian
Tracey, in his "Psychology of Achievement" tapes, says that the
primary factor that ninety three chief executive officers of large
companies attribute to their success is attitude. Another study
elaborated on in the Cox Report indicates that in 1953, the
graduating seniors at Yale were polled to see how many of them
had done any goal setting. It was found that three percent of
them had. Twenty years later, the study found that the three
percent who had set goals was financially worth more than the
entire remainder of the class. So expectations, possibilities,
developmental directions, can bring about great changes in the
world and we need to expect that they can bring about change.

Along with these expectations, however, there needs to be
some acknowledgement or some understanding of the blueprint
of possibilities. This has been lacking in education, both within
schools and at home. The developmental process must be
understood in order to take action for achievement or
fulfillment. To help the child fully participate in his world,

adults must understand where the child is developmentally and what his frame of reference is.

It's been amazing to me as I have worked with people through the years, to find out how many people do not even realize that they think! This gives strong evidence that the stage of concrete operations is still dominating their life. When a person doesn't realize that they think, they are simply taking the results of the environment and acting on it. They are not consciously going through the process of sorting so that they can make choices for themselves. Education today should be acknowledging the inward and the outward values of life.

And how do I know these stages of consciousness exist? Remember back at the beginning, when I mentioned that I made changes in my preschool and my life as a result of a conference I attended? The underlying realities had changed in my life. The changes were not a result of more information or new philosophy. A shift in my fundamental reality, changed my daily living reality.

Here's what happened. At the time I attended this conference, I was at a low point in my life. On the surface, I had much. I was married to a wonderful person, we had a home, I had begun and was successful with a preschool, and I had my degree. Other than having a family, I pretty much had everything society had told me was necessary to be happy and fulfilled. But I wasn't. Inside, I felt devastated and hollow. I didn't know why. My self esteem was so low that, when people said, "Hi, how are you?" my internal response was, "Why are you asking that? You don't care." This was, of course, because I didn't care.

I didn't feel it was okay to have fun, or even to be a social person. I felt I needed to work to justify my being there. So I was off to this church conference to take care of children. One evening the conference program leader, Robert Fulghum, invited me to the evening program of folk dance. I went, and for two or three hours we danced - Greek dance and free-form dance.

As I walked out of there into the warm, night air, I was aware of some change in myself. It was quite intangible at first, yet somehow everything was different! I was seeing, hearing, tasting, touching, and smelling, in a completely new way. The world as I had known it was gone. It was replaced by a world ever so much more enchanting, a world that was fuller in every way.

This meant that everything I was, was more. All my senses were more intense. Colors were deeper, taste and smell more identifiable, sounds more resonant, and touch so much finer. Yet, even as I experienced the senses in a more discriminating, delightful way, there was also a sense of nothing being different at all. Everything was completely connected. It was all part of one whole. To consider the different, separate parts of the world without considering its connection to the whole, was both ludicrous and impossible.

What a joyful experience in life I was having. I never questioned it. It was so natural and wonderful. Actually, what I surmised was that this was what happened when people grew up. I thought I had finally reached adulthood! It took me about two weeks of talking to people about my experience to realize that nothing was farther from the truth. I was not having a common experience.

For about four months I basked in this awareness and then I noticed it was beginning to fade. If I had felt dissatisfied before, now I was really dismayed. I knew that life was wonderful and glorious, and I wanted it that way. Yet, I didn't know where it had come from and how to get it back. I had already changed the course of my life. I had changed lots of daily routines around eating, sleeping, exercise, etc. I gave up the preschool and became a ski instructor. In fact, I started teaching after skiing about sixteen times. You see, when life is seen in unity there is no fear and anything is possible to manifest - so I just did it.

Nevertheless, I was barking up the wrong tree. I was looking for something "out there" to bring back my perspective. Since we are taught that things are created from outside to change the inside, I thought I needed to do something.

A few years and much searching, and the next "accident" happened. One day, on the way to a movie, I changed my plans and went to a Transcendental Meditation talk instead. I decided to do the course, and within three days I knew I was on track to experience unity as a reality in my life.

There were two differences. One was that TM was not doing something outside to change the inside. It was doing something inside to recreate the outside. Second, I began to understand that our perception and experience of the world is due to the functioning of our mind-body system. For some reason, the dancing at that workshop had facilitated a change in my mind-body that gave rise to totally new perceptions. But my system was not able to sustain that style. Within three days of doing TM and getting the meditation information, I began to experience and know something very important. By allowing my mind and body to do nothing without trying to do nothing, this unity experience would be cultured within me as an ongoing, living reality. Like most things, it was a developmental process. Knowledge and experience joined together are great enhancements to life.

My initial experience was like putting 240 volts of electricity through 110 volt wiring. The physical system couldn't handle the high intensity. This was, in my mind, because the coherence that was created kept hitting stress within the physical system. It was like knots on a string that slow down a hand moving along it. Physiologically, these could be biochemical, structural, or energetic.

My sense is that when people have "peak" experiences some internal coherence gets generated, facilitated by something like an event or sensory experience. Yet, because of stress in the physical system, the feelings of the experience don't stay completely intact. Because of our training to look as if things are happening to us from something outside our self, we tend to go on a never-ending adventure to have things change how we feel. What really needs to be done is to stop the doing and allow the being in our experience. Part of this is creating a nervous system that is able to function in a stress-free way to develop and sustain higher consciousness.

Chapter 16

Exploring Inner Space

It is my experience that Transcendental Meditation can make pervasive and significant changes according to nature's priorities.

Thirty years after being introduced to the West, the process of Transcendental Meditation boasts of some of the most prolific research that has been done in any field at any time. More than three hundred fifty research projects in the areas of physiology, psychology, sociology and environment have evaluated what the TM technique has done for individuals and for groups. Even though the research is extensive, and even though large numbers of people have made satisfactory, fulfilling changes in their life by using TM, many people still have an inclination to disregard the technology. This is probably due to an initial bias in Western society against exploring inner space as a way of effectively changing outer space. And so people continue to overlook this process. How many of you just saw the word TM and thought, "Oh, that!" thereby, shutting it off as a possibility? Or maybe you felt that you knew what meditation was and it was definitely not for you. I would like to redefine this technique for you.

TM is an easy, effortless technique that, through the use of sound, allows the mind and body to settle down significantly to levels where change can occur according to nature's priorities.

Very simply, the changes that occur proceed from the levels of rest that are gained. In the previous chapter on stages of consciousness, I described post-representational developmental states that we generally overlook because we do not have role models in our society for these stages of functioning. Now, I'm going to present the process of TM as a way to make changes and approach these states of development. I don't close it off as

We find that the source of all creation, the source of all the atmosphere, the source of all food, drink, and air, and the source of all thinking ability and thought is Being. If there could be a way of communication between our conscious mind and the ocean of Being, that will be the way for conscious atunement with the limitless source of energy.

Maharishi Mahesh Yogi
The Science of Being and the Art of Living,
   p. 163

the *only* possibility. It's just the only possibility I know of that has been validated over and over again on the level of research. In my own experience, I have seen and been acquainted with many people who were able to express these states of consciousness in their own lives, from an experiential, not just an intellectual level.

The TM process is indeed an exploration of inner space. It allows us to understand ourself as the knower, the object to be known, and the process of knowing. It does this by allowing us to take recourse to the natural tendency of the mind to go to greater stages of integration *if* we have some stimulated emission that will allow us to do that.

Systems, left to themselves, go to greater states of entropy. This generally happens in people's lives. They grow to adulthood, don't pay attention to nutrition, do not facilitate the levels of rest they need to carry out dynamic activity, do not continue to grow on the level of gaining information or incorporating new meaning. They become good people who sit and watch television and vegetate until they die -always feeling some little urge inside them that things could be different, but never making that change possible.

TM technique promotes that phase of dynamic rest we need to match the dynamic activity required for working effectively on our wonderful planet. It allows the body to do what it does naturally when it has some time - that is, it rejuvenates itself. When you're sick, a Doctor will give you a prescription, but the universal prescription is "Get some rest." The Doctor realizes that the medication cannot heal, that the cast cannot heal. Only nature, working through its laws on the body, can promote healing. When people take recourse in this deep level of rest, overloads on the physical system are eliminated and the body can begin to function in a better way, first physiologically and then psychologically.

The way change happens is determined by nature. A person might start to meditate to have more mental clarity, for instance, but they might at first notice that they have more energy. This is because nature's priority was to get rid of some of the sluggishness of the functioning of the body. Mental clarity will come, but it will come according to nature's priorities. You just go through the process and let it work.

When I first began my training to teach in the TM program, my first "Ah ha!' was that TM provided a method I could use to intentionally move into the different states of awareness. Before this I could only experience those states sporadically and spontaneously. This gave a lot of satisfaction; it was more like being on a road where there were signs along the way, rather than just going out into the country and beginning to drive. My understanding of the stages of consciousness evaluated and delineated that this was a safe practice for me to engage in.

My second "Ah ha!" was simply that this was an extension of the developmental process. People begin practicing TM wherever they are, developmentally. If they were interrupted or delayed, they simply start tracking where they are. It is a very individual process. No one could really look to another person and use their experiences as an indication as to how TM will unfold in their own life. In fact, that would be a real disadvantage because, in one sense, all of us are on an uncharted highway for our own evolution. Our adventure is to be with the process as a means and an end in itself, and not necessarily to achieve a goal.

I have included in the Appendix some of the studies that show how the process of TM produces change in individuals. Some are from the field of physiology, some from the field of psychology, some from the field of sociology, and some concerning the environment.

A number of research projects have also been done concerning change on the level of consciousness. For instance, Robert Keith Wallace showed that people who were practicing the TM technique were experiencing a different physical process and brain wave pattern than those that were experiencing waking, dreaming or sleeping patterns. This pattern was characterized by an alert mind with a very restful body . It is the physiological condition that I identified as the fourth major state of awareness, or transcendental consciousness.

Many additional studies on the level of brain wave functioning (especially those done by J. D. Bonquet of France), showed that, as a person was meditating initially, there was a spreading of coherency in the brain waves that originated from the back to the front of the head and from side to side. This coherency caused the brain to function as a whole, as an integrated unit. As a person continued to meditate, this experience of brain wave integration was learned by the body as a style of functioning. When it was taken into daily activity, it allowed the person to function in a more integrated, rather than a more chaotic way. This has implications for clarity -- of actually being able to work better under stress rather than the body reverting to the level of survival.

Concerning the other states of awareness that I have described, if the brain is functioning in a more coherent way and the body is also functioning appropriately, we set up the ability for a stage beyond formal operations. That is not only the ability to abstract and to think about thinking, but also the ability to put one's own self in nearly the same perspective as the rest of their environment. This does not mean that the individual ego is eliminated as described in Eastern philosophical literature, but it does mean that our own individuality can be seen in perspective. This is similar to the way a father can see the events of the child's life in perspective and not be completely overwhelmed by them. At this point a person is more capable of moving with the laws of nature rather than being overshadowed by the biases that were previously learned, and it allows freedom in life.

Some people feel that this will cause everyone who uses the technique to act and interact in the same way, and this is quite far from the truth. Individuality certainly remains, and there are always directions that individual prefers to take. However, those directions do not overshadow one's experience; they are just acknowledged and accepted as choices. The difference is that if we have this perspective, rather than becoming overshadowed we have more freedom.

The state of broadened awareness, of maintaining that deep level of silence while we are acting, is possible within the TM experience. Parameters in the lives of people who are practicing the TM program expand in terms of meeting the hierarchy of needs and in terms of being more effective and efficient beings. They increase their opportunities compared with the population in general.

For the sixth and seventh states of awareness, researchers are exploring physiological parameters, as well as how people experiencing these states as a living reality function and interact in their world. Some very exciting research on the biological level has not been identified specifically with states of awareness, but with people that are practicing the TM program. The most basic piece involves a study in Holland with over 2000 meditators. It was found that meditators experienced a significant decrease in nineteen major areas of disease. There have been studies done on the biochemistry in the cells of meditators and non-meditators. Generally speaking, after a very short time of meditating, the biological age of the cells of meditators moves in a very favorable, youthful direction. The cell is more resilient and functions in a more ideal way. These results were found to be positive and long term for people that were practicing the TM program.

Another area where great success was reported is the work that was done with prison populations practicing the TM program. Several of these reports are referenced in the bibliography. Two that come to mind are the program in a women's correctional facility in the state of Vermont, and also in Lampoc Prison in California. People who are incarcerated have extremely high levels of stress. Their stress levels are so high, in fact, that they are not able to see clearly how to respond to accomplish their goals in a way that society will allow. This clouding over of possibilities for appropriate behavior can be attributed to distress -- long term, in many cases -- imposing on the physiological and psychological aspects of that person.

In prison studies, it was found that persons who practiced TM had significantly lower levels of recidivism after release than the prison population as a whole. Most of us are somewhat familiar with the system's seeming inability to rehabilitate people. I would suggest that this has something to do with an imbalance. Rehabilitation cannot be done through teaching some principles. Values must be incorporated in the body at a much more basic level. If there is always a predisposition to follow one's learning bias, these people have learned and used inappropriate responses over most of their lives. TM allows the system to rest and rejuvenate, creating a balanced physical system and opening pathways for change. The psychological effect is that a more positive attitude is gained. So even in one of the most stressed elements of our society, practice of TM promotes long term, positive results.

A supportive physical system and the establishment of coherent brain waves are really necessary for the development and operation of the higher stages of consciousness. It is possible to establish coherent brain waves in several ways, and obviously bio-feedback could be one of them. I do not know if learning to produce coherent brain waves, and then consciously creating coherent waves, produces the same effect as brain waves that are naturally coherent. My guess is that the latter utilizes much less energy because it is a style of functioning that has been incorporated by the body. I am certain that existing within that higher level of development where you can see yourself in relationship to your environment can truly bring about greater stages of freedom, happiness, and enjoyment.

The two highest stages of consciousness are probably too far from most people's experience to be understandable and believable. They certainly do exist in the growth of consciousness and are available for those who allow them to be there. The phrase "allow them" is quite significant and important. Proceeding from our isolated awareness, we use the words development or goal. This assumes there is something "here" and someplace to "go." The development of consciousness, however, is not the same as the infant, toddler, child, adolescent, adult accomplishing two more inches of height or three more words of understanding. The development of consciousness is a natural unfolding. It is allowing the process to happen. But it seems we can set up a configuration to allow this unfolding in a more effective way. We do not go to something, we simply create the balance so that nature can allow us to be who we truly are.

This is very similar to buying a wonderful new TV. When you are in the showroom, the picture and the sound it produces are simply magnificent. You couldn't find something greater at that time. So you purchase the TV set, it arrives, and you turn it on, only to find that neither the sound nor the picture are at that highest level that you saw in the store. You tune it and move the dial here and there and get a little better results, but it still doesn't meet your expectation. You look for the owner's manual and discover that it hasn't been sent. You have to call back to the store to get the manual so you can fine tune it.

When we are born, we don't have a little set of instructions with possibilities and tuning instructions for us as individuals. This is our challenge as human beings. What we need to do, however, is to allow for this machinery of our perception, this wonderful creation of sight and sound, to be all that it is. It's not that we aren't already that, anymore than the TV doesn't have those possibilities incorporated within it. What needs to be done is the balance and the tuning to allow it to be.

This concludes the intervention programs. I have talked about interventions on a much different level than the thinking and talking methods than we have usually experienced. Primary biases may prevent some readers from seriously considering and using these intervention methods. However, I challenge you, particularly on the TM program, to find any other program of overall improvement that can be done as easily and effortlessly, and that has such positive results. Readers who are already involved in other programs might wish to explore some of these areas anyway. Many techniques are not mutually exclusive. The question really is, how far do you want to go in moving through the developmental stages of life toward satisfaction, fulfillment, and enjoyment?

Everyone should know that he is part of
the whole life of the universe and that his
relationship to universal life is what one cell
is to the whole body. If every cell is not
alert, energetic, and healthy, the body as a
whole begins to suffer. Therefore, for the
sake of the life of the individual, and equally
so for the life of everything in the entire
universe, it is necessary that the individual
be healthy, virtuous, good and right in his
every thought, word, and deed. It is a
scientific fact, that the whole universe
reacts to every individual action. The
boundaries of individual life are not
restricted to the boundaries of the body, and
not even to those of one's family or one's
home; they extend far beyond that sphere to
the limitless horizons of cosmic life. Every
action of an individual influences every other
thing in the universe. The universe
influences the individual and the individual
influences the universe. None of them is
independent. One is intimately connected
with the other.

Maharishi Mahesh Yogi
The Science of Being and the Art of Living,
  p. 73

Chapter 17

Conclusion

For most of us, life is unbalanced because we do not experience vertical growth as we obtain horizontal growth. By vertical growth I mean we do not provide for the knower to know herself. We don't explore our inner space while we are gaining facts about our environment (the objects of knowledge). By putting horizontal knowledge together with internal knowledge we create meaning for ourselves.

Readers who are currently involved in parenting or early childhood education will find that their ability to function effectively with children corresponds with their ability to balance horizontal and vertical knowledge.

The first challenge is to create balance in your own life. With consideration for your genetic structure, use nutrition, attitude, exercise, and rest, to keep weak systems from breaking down.

In a book called *Frogs into Princesses*, by Richard Vandler and John Grinder, they relate some fascinating research results. Their subjects were humans, and (of course) that other little animal that we tend to research, laboratory rats. In one experiment, rats and humans were taught to find their way through a maze to achieve a reward. After that maze was accomplished, the reward was taken away. The rats learned to quit doing the maze. The humans didn't.

Isn't that interesting? Even when something doesn't work, humans continue to do it over and over and over again. In this experiment, at least, we do less well than rats in changing our behavior.

The second challenge, then, is that you learn to recognize your established habits and mis-information that have not created for you the outcomes that you want. Recognition will help you to avoid negative or non-productive processes.

The third challenge is to explore and use a broad range of interventions that encourage development in areas that have been interrupted or delayed. You may want to explore further some of the methods I have discussed, such as educational kinesiology, and Transcendental Meditation. The degree to which these interventions allow interrupted or delayed development to become unblocked is dependent on a number of individual factors. However, all of us can make changes that truly will allow movement toward our potential.

Before a child can use the logical abstracting part of the brain to acquire information, he or she must establish an underlying foundation that satisfies their hierarchy of needs. For the prenatal and preschool years, it is necessary to place great priority on comfort, contentment, trust, and security. We need to create within the family system a balance that promotes effective sensory integration so that the schools do not have to be concerned with this area. In the meantime, the schools, whether they wish to or not, should provide at least a support system for that process.

Since the writing of our nation's Constitution, great change has occurred within our society. Much emphasis is placed on the economic and surface values of life. We exist in a frantic cycle of ever-escalating efforts to create satisfaction on a surface level. It is difficult at this time for the education system to intervene in this area. Schools are set up to educate, to give information about our world. We have so little understanding about how to allow knowledge of the self to unfold that we have categorically lumped it into the area of religion and spirituality. It is ignored in the field of education even though we can see that thousands of years of intellectual knowledge and technological advancement haven't solved the basic problems of humans.

Recently, I was discussing these issues with a school superintendent who was on a national committee for the development of creative thinking, and he agreed that the school was originally intended to educate the logical abstracting brain. I asked him how we should help students develop their creative thinking process. He said he believes that there is a stated curriculum and a hidden curriculum in every area of classroom education. Within the stated curriculum, students need more time to explore their subjects, rather than just provide right and wrong answers.

He then went on to talk about the hidden curriculum, which has to do with life situations in school, such as when a student behaves inappropriately. Are they just punished and that is it? Or are they given the ability to learn - to think creatively about their behavior? The child who does not behave appropriately should be encouraged to review and consider alternatives for that particular behavior. In other words, the *message* of the school about the value of creative thinking is important.

In education, there always seems to be a time crunch to complete the curriculum, to teach for the test. I suggest that this is a self-imposed, inappropriate mode of learning. In New Zealand, students are not evaluated until the eighth or ninth grade, at which time they consistently rank very high in the whole world in terms of their ability to express and use information.

We could change our style of thinking. With some insight we could move to a program with less concrete styles of evaluating what is right and wrong. We could move beyond simply using information as a standard of knowledge about our external world.

As a more appropriate standard, we could move toward meaning and the expression of values in daily life. We currently give a lot of information to students without allowing them to incorporate meanings for themselves. We tell young people how and what to do in life without allowing them to learn.

Recalling Rudolph Driekurs' work on logical consequences, we need to allow the child, on a day to day basis, to discover the consequences of his behavior so that he can learn how life is functioning for him. Additionally, we need to provide support for him so that he feels free to make changes where things are not working out.

The educator has to be a very flexible person. At a minimum, the educator should have achieved the level of formal operations. Ideally, educators with a bachelor's degree would have achieved the stage of Cosmic Consciousness. Movement to Refined Cosmic Consciousness would be accomplished at the master's level, and a person with a Ph.D. would be firmly in the stage of Unity Consciousness.

We must make sure that three parts of learning are explored: the knower, the object of knowledge, and the process of knowing. When these three areas are in balance, learning takes place in a spontaneous, effortless way. Remember that by age seven, we know eighty percent of everything we're ever going to know except for specific facts. How many formal learning situations were set up to create that? It happens spontaneously, according to developmental capabilities and through interaction with the environment.

We have moved from the beginning of time through collective understandings. A great momentum has been gained toward an understanding of the basic processes that bring non-existence into existence. Some concepts on the leading edge of physics express this most clearly. The intellect's capability of bringing forth such a delightful understanding will go far toward satisfying our yearning for knowledge. And yet, the other part of this is that we should have the *experiential* reality of knowing non-existence coming into existence on a day to day basis, on a moment to moment basis.

Different philosophies, different theories, different ideas throughout history, have given human beings a collective awareness of how the world functions. Collectively, at the end of this Twentieth century we stand on the brink of being able to literally explode our consciousness and unfold a heaven on earth. We have the information and we have the tools to allow this to happen. If we use both of those in a balanced way, each individual should be able to experience life unfolding at its highest level.

Appendix

The following charts were taken from the Collected Papers, Volume 1 of *Scientific Research on the Trancendental Meditation Program*, edited by David Orme-Johnson and John T. Farrow, and from Volume 2, edited by Roger Chalmers and Geoffrey Clements.

PHYSIOLOGICAL FUNCTIONING

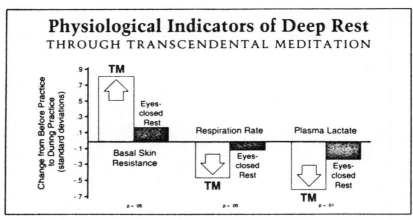

Physiological Indicators of Deep Rest
THROUGH TRANSCENDENTAL MEDITATION

A meta-analysis, the preferred scientific procedure for drawing definitive conclusions from large bodies of research, found Maharishi's Transcendental Meditation technique produced a significant increase in basal skin resistance compared to eyes-closed rest, indicating profound relaxation. Deep rest and relaxation were also indicated by greater decreases in respiration rates and plasma lactate levels compared to ordinary rest. These physiological changes occur spontaneously as the mind effortlessly settles to the state of restful alertness, transcendental consciousness.

References: 1. *American Psychologist* 42 (1987): 879–881.
2. *Science* 167 (1970): 1751–1754.
3. *American Journal of Physiology* 221 (1971): 795–799.

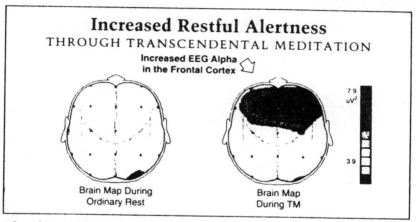

The electroencephalograph brain maps above illustrate the findings of several studies that Maharishi's Transcendental Meditation technique increases the EEG index of restful alertness—increased slow alpha frequency power in the frontal cortex. This change in the EEG indicates a relaxed state of wakefulness during Transcendental Meditation, an ordered state of brain functioning that is ideal preparation for dynamic activity.

References: 1. *Science* 167 (1970): 1751–1754.
2. *Scientific American* 226 (1972): 84–90.
3. *American Journal of Physiology* 221 (1971): 795–799.
4. *Electroencephalography and Clinical Neurophysiology* 35 (1973): 143–151.

MENTAL POTENTIAL

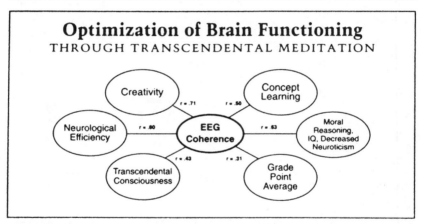

Optimization of Brain Functioning
THROUGH TRANSCENDENTAL MEDITATION

Higher levels of EEG coherence measured during the practice of Maharishi's Transcendental Meditation technique are significantly correlated with increased fluency of verbal creativity, increased efficiency in learning new concepts, more principled moral reasoning, higher verbal IQ, decreased neuroticism, clearer experiences of transcendental consciousness, and increased neurological efficiency, as measured by faster recovery of the H-reflex.

References: The chart above was constructed with data from the following four studies:
1. *International Journal of Neuroscience* 13 (1981): 211-217.
2. *International Journal of Neuroscience* 15 (1981): 151-157.
3. *Scientific Research on the Transcendental Meditation Program: Collected Papers. Volume 1* (Livingston Manor, NY: MERU Press, 1977), paper 21, 208-212.
4. *Scientific Research on Maharishi's Transcendental Meditation and TM-Sidhi Programme: Collected Papers, Volume 4* (the Netherlands: MVU Press, 1989), paper 294, 2245-2266.

SCIENTIFIC RESEARCH ON MAHARISHI'S
TRANSCENDENTAL MEDITATION AND TM-SIDHI PROGRAM

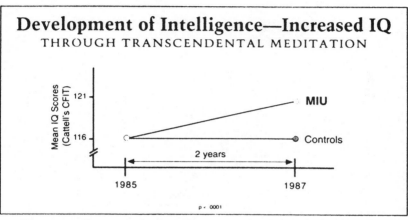

Development of Intelligence—Increased IQ
THROUGH TRANSCENDENTAL MEDITATION

Students at Maharishi International University (MIU) in Fairfield, Iowa, U.S.A., who regularly practiced Maharishi's Transcendental Meditation and TM-Sidhi program over a two-year period increased significantly in intelligence and ability to make rapid choice decisions compared to control subjects from another Iowa university. This finding corroborates other studies showing increased IQ and faster choice reaction through Transcendental Meditation.

References: 1. *Personality and Individual Differences* 12 (1991): 1105–1116.
2. *Perceptual and Motor Skills* 62 (1986): 731–738.
3. *College Student Journal* 15 (1981): 140–146.
4. *The Journal of Creative Behavior* 19 (1985): 270–275.
5. *Journal of Clinical Psychology* 42 (1986): 161–164.
6. *Gedrag: Tijdschrift voor Psychologie* [Behavior: Journal of Psychology] 3 (1975): 167–182.

EDUCATION

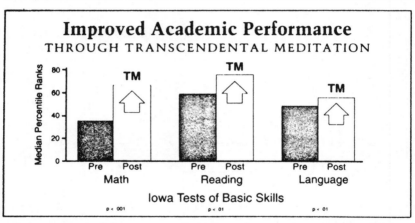

Improved Academic Performance
THROUGH TRANSCENDENTAL MEDITATION

Iowa Tests of Basic Skills

After one year of practice of Maharishi's Transcendental Meditation program, elementary school students showed significant gains on the Iowa Tests of Basic Skills, a nationally standardized test (ref. 1). A second study showed significant gains in high school students (grades 9–12) on the Iowa Tests of Educational Development (ref. 2). A third study (ref. 3) found that the length of time students had been practicing the Transcendental Meditation program was significantly correlated with academic achievement, independent of student IQ scores.

References: 1. *Education* 107 (1986): 49–54.
2. *Education 109* (1989). 302–304.
3. *Modern Science and Vedic Science* 1 (1987): 433–468.

SCIENTIFIC RESEARCH ON MAHARISHI'S
TRANSCENDENTAL MEDITATION AND TM-SIDHI PROGRAM

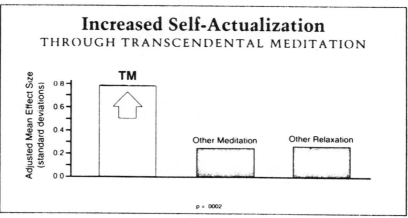

Increased Self-Actualization
THROUGH TRANSCENDENTAL MEDITATION

Statistical meta-analysis of all available studies (42 independent outcomes) indicated that the effect of Maharishi's Transcendental Meditation program on increasing self-actualization is much greater than that of other forms of meditation and relaxation. Self-actualization refers to realizing more of one's inner potential, expressed in every area of life: integration and stability of personality, self-regard, emotional maturity, capacity for warm interpersonal relationships, and adaptive response to challenges.

References: 1. *Journal of Social Behavior and Personality* 6 (1991): 189-247.
2. *Higher Stages of Human Development: Perspectives on Adult Growth*
(New York: Oxford University Press, 1990), 286–341.
3. *Journal of Counseling Psychology* 19 (1972): 184-187.

HEALTH

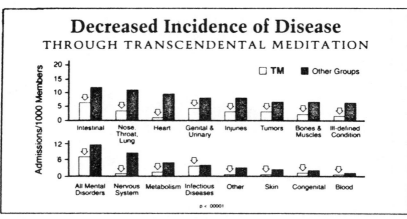

Decreased Incidence of Disease
THROUGH TRANSCENDENTAL MEDITATION

p < 00001

A five-year study of medical care utilization statistics on 2,000 people throughout the U.S. who regularly practiced Maharishi's Transcendental Meditation and TM-Sidhi program found that their overall rate of hospitalization was 56% lower than the norm. The group practicing Transcendental Meditation had fewer hospital admissions in all disease categories compared to the norm—including 87% less hospitalization for cardiovascular disease, 55% less for cancer, 87% less for diseases of the nervous system, and 73% less for nose, throat, and lung problems.

Reference: 1 *Psychosomatic Medicine* 49 (1987). 493-507.

SCIENTIFIC RESEARCH ON MAHARISHI'S
TRANSCENDENTAL MEDITATION AND TM-SIDHI PROGRAM

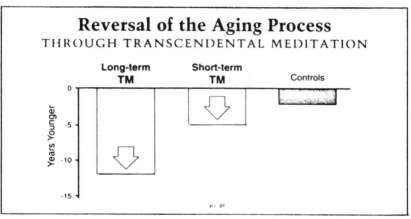

Reversal of the Aging Process
THROUGH TRANSCENDENTAL MEDITATION

Biological age measures how old a person is physiologically. As a group, long-term meditators who had been practicing Maharishi's Transcendental Meditation program for more than 5 years were physiologically 12 years younger than their chronological age, as measured by lower blood pressure, and better near-point vision and auditory discrimination. Short-term meditators were physiologically 5 years younger than their chronological age. The study statistically controlled for the effects of diet and exercise.

References: 1. *International Journal of Neuroscience* 16 (1982): 53-58.
2. *Journal of Personality and Social Psychology* 57 (1989): 950-964.
3. *AGE* 10 (1987): 160.

MAHARISHI AYUR-VED

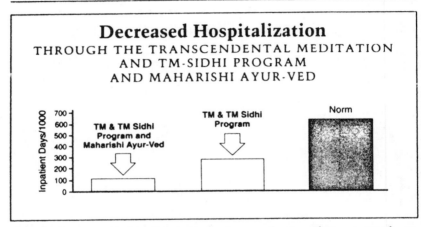

Decreased Hospitalization
THROUGH THE TRANSCENDENTAL MEDITATION
AND TM-SIDHI PROGRAM
AND MAHARISHI AYUR-VED

Maharishi Ayur-Ved is the most ancient and scientific system of natural medicine, which uses a variety of approaches that influence all levels of life simultaneously—consciousness, physiology, behavior, and environment—to maintain health and promote longevity. Health insurance statistics showed that people who practiced Maharishi's Transcendental Meditation and TM-Sidhi program were hospitalized 56% less than the norm. A second study found that people who participated in other Maharishi Ayur-Ved prevention programs in addition to the Transcendental Meditation and TM-Sidhi program were hospitalized 84% less than the norm.

References: 1. *Psychosomatic Medicine* 49 (1987): 493-507.
2. *Journal of the Iowa Academy of Science* 95(1)(1988): A56.

SCIENTIFIC RESEARCH ON MAHARISHI'S
TRANSCENDENTAL MEDITATION AND TM-SIDHI PROGRAM

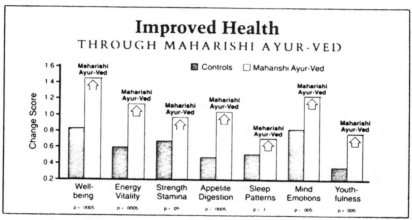

This study found that people who participated in a Maharishi Ayur-Ved physiological purification program for one week improved significantly in general well-being, energy and vitality, strength and stamina, appetite and digestive patterns, state of mind and emotions, and youthfulness and rejuvenation. Control subjects who received only intellectual knowledge of Maharishi Ayur-Ved for the same amount of time did not show the same amount of improvement. These findings indicate that the Maharishi Ayur-Ved purification program promotes physiological and psychological balance.

Reference: 1. The Journal of Social Behavior and Personality 5 (1990): 1-27.

SOCIAL BEHAVIOR

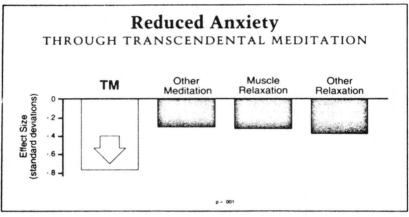

Meta-analysis is a scientific procedure for drawing definitive con-clusions from large bodies of research, systematically combining the results of many studies. A statistical meta-analysis conducted at Stanford University of all available studies (146 independent outcomes) indicated that the effect of Maharishi's Transcendental Meditation program on reducing trait anxiety was much greater than that of all other meditation and relaxation techniques, including progressive muscle relaxation. Analysis showed that these positive results could not be attributed to subject expecta-tion, experimenter bias, or quality of research design.

References: 1. *Journal of Clinical Psychology* 45 (1989): 957–974.
2. *Journal of Clinical Psychology* 33 (1977): 1076-1078.

SCIENTIFIC RESEARCH ON MAHARISHI'S
TRANSCENDENTAL MEDITATION AND TM-SIDHI PROGRAM

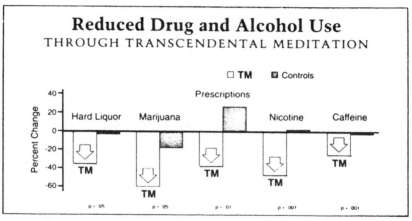

Reduced Drug and Alcohol Use
THROUGH TRANSCENDENTAL MEDITATION

A random sample of practitioners of Maharishi's Transcendental Meditation program and matched control subjects found that after an average of 19 months practicing Transcendental Meditation, usage levels of all substances declined significantly, while usage levels of controls did not change over the same period. Length of time meditating and regularity of meditation were positively correlated with decreased substance usage (ref. 1). Twenty-four studies have consistently found that the Transcendental Meditation program reduces use of all categories of drugs (refs. 2 and 3).

References: 1. *International Journal of the Addictions* 12 (1977): 729–754.
2. *American Journal of Psychiatry* 131 (1974): 60–63.
3. *International Journal of the Addictions* 26 (1991): 293–325.

BUSINESS

Improved Health Among the Work Force
THROUGH TRANSCENDENTAL MEDITATION

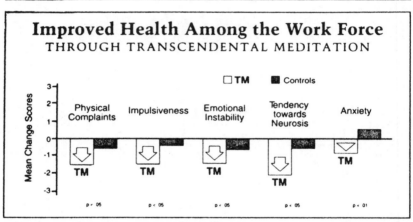

In a large study conducted by the Japanese National Institute of Health, 447 industrial workers of Sumitomo Heavy Industries were taught Maharishi's Transcendental Meditation technique and compared with 321 non-meditating workers over a 5-month period. The Transcendental Meditation group showed significant decreases in physical complaints, impulsiveness, emotional instability, neurotic tendencies, and anxiety, as well as decreased insomnia and smoking.

References: 1. *Japanese Journal of Industrial Health* 32 (1990): 656.
2. *Japanese Journal of Public Health* 37 (1990): 729.

SCIENTIFIC RESEARCH ON MAHARISHI'S
TRANSCENDENTAL MEDITATION AND TM-SIDHI PROGRAM

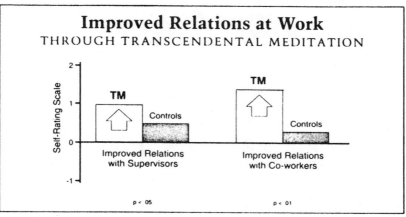

Improved Relations at Work
THROUGH TRANSCENDENTAL MEDITATION

Employees practicing Maharishi's Transcendental Meditation program an average of 11 months showed significant improvements at work compared with members of a control group. Relationships with co-workers and supervisors improved, and job performance and job satisfaction increased, while the desire to change jobs decreased (ref. 1). The results of this research were replicated in a study with several control groups, which also found significant improvements in the same areas (ref. 2).

References: 1. *Academy of Management Journal* 17 (1974): 362–368.
2. *Scientific Research on the Transcendental Meditation Program: Collected Papers,* Volume 1 (Livingston Manor, NY: MERU Press, 1977), paper 97, 630–638.

REHABILITATION

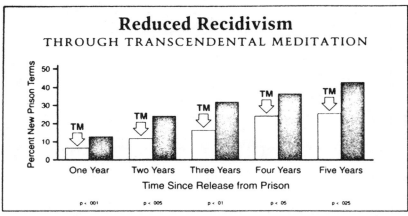

Reduced Recidivism
THROUGH TRANSCENDENTAL MEDITATION

In this study, 259 male felon parolees of the California Department of Corrections who learned the Transcendental Meditation technique while in prison had fewer new prison terms and more favorable parole outcomes each year over a five-year period after release compared to carefully matched controls. The Transcendental Meditation program was shown to significantly reduce recidivism during a period of six months to six years after parole, whereas prison education, vocational training, and psychotherapy did not consistently reduce recidivism.

References: 1. *Journal of Criminal Justice* 15 (1987): 211–230.
2. *Dissertation Abstracts International* 43 (1982): 539B.
3. *International Journal of Comparative and Applied Criminal Justice* 11 (1987): 111–132.

SCIENTIFIC RESEARCH ON MAHARISHI'S
TRANSCENDENTAL MEDITATION AND TM-SIDHI PROGRAM

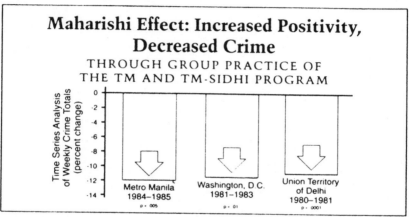

Maharishi Effect: Increased Positivity, Decreased Crime
THROUGH GROUP PRACTICE OF THE TM AND TM-SIDHI PROGRAM

During periods when groups practicing Maharishi's Transcendental Meditation and TM-Sidhi program exceeded the square root of one percent of the population, crime decreased in Metro Manila, Philippines (mid-August 1984 to late January 1985); Washington, D.C. (October 1981 to October 1983); and the Union Territory of Delhi, India (November 1980 to March 1981). Analysis verified that these decreases in crime could not have been due to trends or cycles in the data, or to changes in police policies and procedures.

References: 1. The Journal of Mind and Behavior 8 (1987): 67–104.
2. The Journal of Mind and Behavior 9 (1988): 457–486.

Growing Up Inside Out

BIBLIOGRAPHY

Alexander, C. N., et al. "Growth of Higher Stages of Consciousness: Maharishi's Vedic Psychology of Human Development." In *Higher Stages of Human Development,* edited by C.N. Alexander and E.J. Langer. New York: Oxford University Press, 1990.

Auel, Jean. *Clan of the Cave Bear. New York. Bantam.*

Ayres, A. Jean. *Sensory Integration and the Child.* Los Angeles, Western Psychological Services, 1979.

Bandler, Richard, Grinder, John. *Frogs Into Princes.* Moab, Utah: Real People Press, 1979.

Bach, Richard. *The Bridge Across Forever.* New York: William Morson Co., 1984.

Bach, Richard. *Illusions.* New York: Dell Publishing Co., Inc. 1977.

Bach, Richard. *Johnathon Livingston Seagull.* New York: Macmillan, 1970.

Briggs, John, and Peat, F.David. *Looking Glass Universe.* New York: Simon & Schuster, Inc., 1984.

Campbell, Anthony. *TM and the Nature of Enlightenment.* New York: Harper & Row, 1975.

Capra, Fritjof. *The Tao of Physics.* New York: Bantam Books, 1975.

Chalmers, Roger, and Clements, Geoffrey. (ed.) *Scientific Research on the Transcendental Meditation Program; Collected Papers, Volume 1.* Seelisburg, Switzerland, Maharishi European Research University Press, 1977.

Cheraskin, E., Ringsdorf, W. M., and Clark, J. W. *Diet and Disease*. New Canaan, Conn: Keats Publishing Co., 1975.

Chopra, Deepak. *Ageless Body, Timeless Mind*. New York, Harmony Books, 1993.

Chopra, Deepak. *Perfect Health*. New York, Harmony Books, 1985.

Chopra, Deepak. *Quantum Healing*. New York, Bantam Books, 1985.

Chopra, Deepak. *Unconditional Life: mastering the forces that shape reality*. New York: Bantam Books, 1991.

Chuang-tzu. *Inner Chapters*. New York, Vintage Press, 1974.

Colorado Department of Education. *Training of Trainers*. Denver, Colorado: CDE & NCBOCS, 1988.

Cousins, Norman. *Anatomy of an Illness*. New York, Bantam Books, 1989.

Dennison, Paul E. and Dennison, Gail E. *Brain Gym: Simple Activities for Whole Brain Learning*. Glendale, California, Edu-Kinesthetics, Inc. 1986

Dunne, Lavoni. *The Nutritional Almanac*. New York, McGraw-Hill, 1990.

Ellsworth, Peter, and Sindt, Vincent. *Implementing a Developmental Thinking Skills Curriculum*. National Curriculum Study Institutes, Association for Supervision and Curriculum Development, Alexandria, Virginia: 1988.

Ferguson, Marilyn. *The Aquarian Conspiracy: Personal and Social Transformation in the 1980s*. Los Angeles, J.P. Tarcher, Inc. 1980.

Fulghum, Robert, *All I Really Need To Know I Learned in Kindergarten*. New York: Random House, Ballantine Books, 1986.

Gibran, Khalil. *The Prophet*. New York: Alfred A.Knopf, Inc., 1923.

Grady, Michael P., and Luecke, Emily. *Education and the Brain*. Bloomington, Indiana, Phi Delta Kappa Educational Foundation, 1978.

Hoffman, Banesh. *The Strange Story of the Quantum*. Dover, New York: 1959.

Maharishi International University. *Modern Science and Vedic Science*. Maharishi International University, Fairfield, Iowa: 1987.

Maharishi Mahesh Yogi, in Jn. of Modern Science and Vedic Science, p. 472. quoted from American Association for Ideal Education, 1985, p. 5.

Maharishi Mahesh Yogi. *On the Baghavad Gita: a new translation and commentary*.Baltimore, Maryland, Penguin Books, Inc., 1969.

Maharishi Mahesh Yogi, *The Science of Creative Intelligence*. International Symposium on the Science of Creative Intelligence, Maharishi International University, 1972.

Maharishi Mahesh Yogi. *The Science of Being and the Art of Living*. New York: Signet, 1963.

Montessori, Maria. *The Secrets of Childhood*. New York: Random House, Ballantine Books, 1966.

Orme-Johnson, David, and Farrow, John T. (ed.) *Scientific Research on the Transcendental Meditation Program; Collected Papers, Volume 2.* Seelisburg, Switzerland, Maharishi European Research University Press, 1989.

Ornstein, Robert, and Sobel, David. *The Healing Brain.* New York: Simon and Schuster, 1987.

Pearce, Joseph Chilton. *The Magical Child.* New York: Bantam Books, 1986.

Perkins, David N, *Teaching Creative Thinking.* National Curriculum Study Institutes, Association for Supervision and Curriculum Development., Alexandria, Virginia: 1988.

Pfieffer, Carl C. *Mental and Elemental Nutrients.* New Canaan Conn: Keats Publishing Co., 1975.

Raine, Kathleen. *The Land Unknown.* New York: Braziller, 1975.

Smith, Landon. *Improving Your Child's Behavioral Chemistry.*Englewood Cliffs, N.J.: Prentice-Hall, 1976.

Sternberg, Robert J. *Teaching Critical Thinking: Eight Easy Ways To Fail Before You Begin.*

Swanson, Gerald, and Oates, Robert. *Enlightened Management: Buiding High-Performance People.* Fairfield, Iowa: Maharishi International University Press, 1989.

Tracey, Brian. Psychology of Achievement. (tapes) Nightingale-Connant.

Vandler, Richard, and Grinder, John. *Frogs Into Princesses.* Moab, Utah, Real People Press, 1979.

Vitale, Barbara Meister. *Unicorns Are Real: a right brained approach to learning.* New York, Warner Books, 1982.

INDEX

Index

emotional brain, 29, 44, 93
    during stress response, 52, 65
    in psychotherapy, 73
emotions, in decision-making, 79
empirical information, using to evaluate techniques, 70
entropy, 128
environment, perceiving through senses, 12
equilibration, 77
expectations, explaining to the child, 65, 67
experience,
    as a learning process, 70, 109
    importance in learning, 23
Ferguson, Marilyn, 73
field theory, 89
formal operations, stage of, 25,
Fulghum, Robert, 1, 32, 123
Gelderlios, Paul, 57
Gibran, Khalil, 43
Grady, Michael P., 39 97
gravity, sense of, development and function, 18
Grinder, John, 135
habits, recognizing, 135
healing, and rest, 128
hierarchy of stages, 3
holding the infant to enhance development, 37-38
holistic view, 24
horizontal knowledge, 58
immune system, reactions under stress, 50-51
intellect, 12, 27
intuition, 11, 26,
    mother's, 38
intuitive information, using to evaluate techniques, 70
knowledge,
    objective, 104
    subjective, 104
Langer, E. J., 107-114, 116-117, 119-122
lateralization, 21
    facilities developed, 24

163